For Maureen & N.
as a token of

STOREY
A Priest for his Time

Peter Roebuck

BOOKCASE

Other books by Peter Roebuck

Yorkshire Baronets 1640-1760: Families, Estates & Fortunes (Oxford, 1980).

The Foundation Decade at Shrigley: Seminary, Church & Shrine (Rome, 2004).

Cattle Droving, Cotton & Landownership: A Cumbrian Family Saga (Kendal, 2014).

Cattle Droving through Cumbria 1600-1900 (Carlisle, 2015)

As Contributing Editor:

Constable of Everingham Estate Correspondence 1726-43 (Yorks. A.S.R.S. 1974).

Plantation to Partition: Essays in Ulster History (Belfast, 1981)

Public Service & Private Fortune: The Life of Lord Macartney 1737-1806 (Belfast, 1983).

Economy & Society in Scotland & Ireland 1500-1939 (with R.M. Mitchison, Edinburgh, 1988).

The University of Ulster: Genesis & Growth (with G. O'Brien, Dublin, 2009)

Copyright: Peter Roebuck
First edition 2019
ISBN 978-1-912181-24-7
Published by Bookcase, 19 Castle St., Carlisle, CA3 8SY
01228 544560 bookscumbria@aol.com
Printed by The Amadeus Press.

'I never really found myself enamoured of the clerical set-up, I must say, and so I always felt slightly an outsider.'

(Storey, Memoir, 2005)

For my grandsons
Obi, Dara, Oscar & Kit

Frontispiece: Storey in his early 20s,
St. Mary's Hall, Stonyhurst, early 1940s

CONTENTS

List of Illustrations

Preface

Fr. Anthony Joseph Storey lived for 88 years and remained extraordinarily active for all but the last few weeks of his long life. Born in 1919 into a well-heeled, rural, upper-middle class Catholic family in the East Riding of Yorkshire, he was privately educated before proceeding in 1936 to train for the priesthood at the English College in Rome. In 1940 he and a College friend narrowly escaped serious trouble after tearing down Fascist posters in the centre of the city. A few days later, when Italy entered the war, he and all his fellow seminarians were hastily evacuated, travelling on the last train from Rome to Paris as the German army overran the French border; and catching the last ferry to Southampton before the harbour at Le Havre was mined. Having completed his studies at St. Mary's Hall, Stonyhurst, he was ordained for the diocese of Middlesbrough in 1943 aged 24. Unusually, he was then sent by his bishop to study for a degree in History at the University of Cambridge. Thereafter, he worked as a curate for almost two decades in Middlesbrough and Hull, two of Britain's most deprived urban areas. For a decade from 1962 he served as the first full-time Catholic Chaplain at the University of Hull, an exciting, indeed tumultuous experience which left him exhausted and glad to move on. He was then appointed Parish Priest in a variety of locations in north and east Yorkshire, notably for 15 years at Holy Cross in Cottingham. Although he retired from there in 1996 aged 77, he remained active as a priest until shortly before his death in 2007.

His lifetime witnessed profound changes in virtually every

facet of human life, not least in Catholicism and the Catholic Church. Anthony Storey was fiercely loyal to his faith and to the Church he served. He was also a well-educated and highly intelligent man of a distinctly independent and questing cast of mind. While not always easy to reconcile, these two characteristics provided fertile ground for the growth of an inspired ministry which, in turbulent times, was deeply appreciated, especially by lay people, and he won a very large following. In addition to describing his long and influential career, this book endeavours to trace the origins and nature of the many strands of his complex personality, attitudes and outlook; to identify significant junctures in his life; and to chart the process whereby key influences coalesced to inform and enrich a remarkable priestly ministry and a profound personal wisdom. It describes how one priest successfully negotiated the challenges of his times.

One matter requires explanation. Throughout what follows Fr. Storey is simply called Storey, which is how cohorts of students, I among them, knew him as Chaplain at the University of Hull. We have never been able to call him anything else. As one of his many friends explained: 'despite having known him for well over 40 years, we still call him Storey; and every time we try to escape this habit, we end up with the same name, which was, and is, a positive term of endearment'.

I wish to thank the very many individuals who have helped me with this book. I am grateful to the diocese of Middlesbrough for access to its archives and, in particular, to its archivist, David Smallwood, for his guidance. Storey's father, George, and his brother, Peter, both attended Ushaw College and Anne Timothy kindly assisted me with the archives there. Adrian Allan and the late Dr. R. Yorke provided me with valuable material on Bishop's Court at Freshfield, Storey's prep school. David Knight, archivist at Stonyhurst College, could not have been more helpful in charting my way through the College records; Jan Graffius, the Curator, introduced me to a key deposit, Storey's photograph album; and my understanding of Jesuit education was furthered by Fr. John Fairhurst S.J. I was granted access to the archives of the Venerable English College in Rome by the Rector, Monsignor Philip Whitmore. Fortunately, I began working on that episode in Storey's life just as Professor Maurice Whitehead, a long-standing friend of his, began his labour of cataloguing the College archives. I am especially grateful for his help. The Master, Professor Jane Stapleton, and the Fellows of Christ's College, Cambridge kindly permitted me to search their records and in doing so I was generously assisted by the Librarian, John Wagstaff, and by two of his colleagues, James Smith and Charlotte Hoare.

I am greatly indebted to the many friends and former colleagues of Storey who shared with me their personal records and memories of him. Chief among these were Marian Hall and her husband, Steve, with whom Storey left a large corpus of records and papers which I was able to examine over many months. I was also free to interrogate Marian's unrivalled knowledge of Storey's life during his last twenty-five years. Among those who responded to my queries were the current Bishop of Middlesbrough, the Rt. Revd. Terence Drainey, his immediate predecessor, Emeritus Bishop John Crowley, and Fr. Peter Keeling who delivered the appreciation at Storey's funeral. Valuable testimony and records were provided by very many others too numerous to mention, but especially by Margaret Blatchford, Barbara Cunningham, Barbara Hungin, Christina Lucey, Emrys Hughes, Veronica Prattley and Teresa Ulyatt. In addition to the information they provided, I am grateful for lively discussions with two of Storey's nephews, Peter and Michel Knapton, the sons of his sister, Agatha.

As the book grew I benefited greatly from further

information and comments on successive drafts by colleagues and friends. Especially valuable were those from Eamon Duffy, a close friend of Storey, who saved me from sundry misinterpretations and helped me to find a tone for the book. There were also valuable contributions from Norma Birley, Tony Carew, Bruce Kent, Mark Lambert, Michael Mullett, Gerry O'Brien and John Sullivan. None of these is responsible for the views expressed here or for the overall interpretation. Responsibility for them is mine alone.

My wife, Fiona, knew Storey for almost as long as I did and he married us in 1968. As always but especially while working on this book, I have had her unfailing support and the benefit of her wise judgement. She has my warmest thanks.

Peter Roebuck
Penrith, Cumbria
peter.roebuck3@gmail.com

December 2018

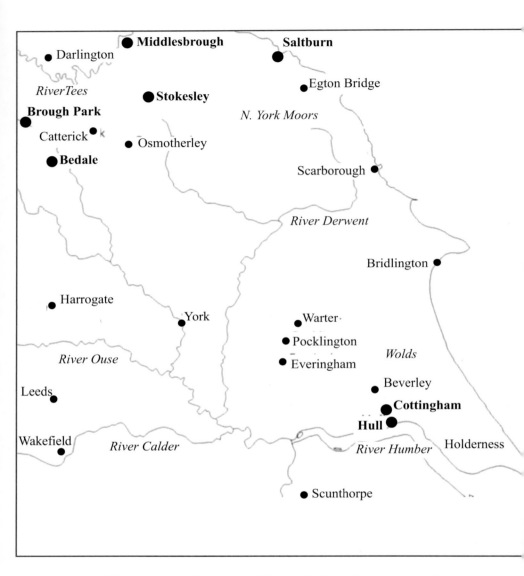

1: *Map showing location of Storey's Appointments in the Diocese of Middlesbrough, given in* **Bold Type***, with other significant locations mentioned in the text.*

INTRODUCTION

In east Yorkshire Wednesday 9 May 2007 was cloudy and overcast with intermittent rain. It was an unpromising spring day and the centre of the city of Hull was sparsely populated for most of the morning. Towards midday a crowd began to gather for a funeral in the church of St. Charles Borromeo in Jarratt Street, the main place of Catholic worship in the city. The numbers grew steadily and gradually moved inside the building. Long before the service began the large church, normally seating up to 500, was full to capacity: people were standing as well as sitting in the body of the church and in the choir loft; those unable to get in gathered outside on the steps and in the street. Ultimately, the size of the crowd approached and perhaps exceeded a thousand. This extraordinarily large congregation had gathered in the sort of numbers we associate with funerals of the great and the good, of show-business celebrities or major politicians, or with the tragic or untimely death of the very young. The occasion, however, was the funeral of a blind, 88 year old Catholic priest, Fr. Anthony Storey, who had never held major ecclesiastical or public office, and who had retired from official ministry more than a decade earlier.

There had been five brothers and two sisters in Storey's family but only two were still alive: John, an older brother, had lived in Australia for years and could not attend; and Patience, a younger sister, was in the front pew of the church. All had been brought up to be sturdily independent. Despite having lived a very different life from him, based in the south of England and with lots of foreign travel, Patience felt a special affinity with Anthony (or 'Ant', as they all called him) because he was the youngest son and she the youngest daughter. Not knowing how many people were expected at the service, she looked round the church at regular intervals before it began, and at one point asked a neighbour what on earth all the fuss was about. She was astonished by the sheer number of those who wanted to attend her brother's funeral.

In one capacity or another Storey had served the diocese of Middlesbrough for over half a century: but, though he was a man of immense personal charisma, first-class intelligence and rock-like integrity, who would certainly have risen to the highest levels of any other profession, his superiors had never promoted him. Many of the people who gathered to honour him that day must have reflected on this puzzling fact. Most of them were there because they believed Storey to have been the finest priest and one of the most remarkable human beings they had ever encountered. For many of them he had loomed even larger, a major influence not only on their religious beliefs but on the conduct of their lives.

Originally from Northumberland, most, though not all, of Storey's forbears had been staunchly Catholic. His faith, therefore, was inherited: he was a cradle Catholic. He cherished his pedigree and kept in touch with relatives in the far north of England and elsewhere throughout his life. His loyalty to the Catholic Church was fierce and unassailable, and he paid tribute to two powerful, familial influences on it: what he had learned at his mother's knee; and what he had imbibed of his father's knowledge of early European history, especially of northern monasticism. Yet unusually, even among his own family and certainly among many of his co-religionists, all this co-existed, apparently without any sense of strain, with a questioning mind, a mind which refused to take his inheritance for granted or as the last word. For him Catholicism was based on an age-old faith: but it was also a living, moving thing, and he lived and moved with it. Beliefs were not cast in stone: they progressed and the faithful grew in understanding and interpretation of them, and should never be frightened of doing so.

Some years earlier, at the funeral of his older sister, Agatha, Storey had suggested that obstinacy was something which he and his siblings had in common. He also revealed that, according to one exasperated bishop, he was especially guilty of it. Later, Agatha's son, Michael, speaking at Patience's funeral, felt that Storey had been referring to a far more complex trait: to 'something decidedly less negative [than obstinacy]; having strong feelings and strong convictions, the latter honestly thought through; [and] sticking by them'. Storey was relentless in his quest to understand and get to the bottom of things, especially in regard to his faith. In striving to do so he frequently articulated what was for him a core conviction: a clear distinction should be drawn between one's loyalty to the Church and what one believed on the one hand, and one's feelings about the people temporarily in charge of the institution on the other.

Having trained for the priesthood in Rome, he kept closely in touch with developments there; he was a prompt and careful reader of Vatican news, papal encyclicals and Council documents; and he paid warm tribute to how much he admired many of them, and how they had guided his behaviour as a priest. But his deep loyalty to the Church did not blind him to the reality that clerics, however exalted, were fallible human beings. They could make mistakes, of interpretation, emphasis, response or other behaviour; and in his view quite often did so. This attitude was underpinned by what, for a cleric, was a rare and lifelong scepticism about the nature of the clerical state. 'I never really found myself enamoured of the clerical set-up, I must say, and so I always felt slightly an outsider.' This was no ordinary man and certainly no conventional priest.

In part at least, his outlook derived from his distinctive upbringing, privileged education, and sharp intellect. For rather longer than most children Storey was insulated from institutional influences and educated at home by his mother. Subsequently, like most of his brothers before him, he was sent to Bishop's Court, a Catholic Preparatory School at Freshfield in Lancashire; and afterwards he went further north to Stonyhurst , the boarding school run by the Jesuits. His early studies for the Middlesbrough diocesan priesthood were at the English College in Rome but, following the repatriation of the College just before Italy entered the war in 1940, they continued and were completed at St. Mary's Hall, Stonyhurst. Then came a totally unexpected opportunity: after his ordination in 1943 the bishop sent him to Christ's College, Cambridge to study for a degree in History. Thus, in Storey's case intellectual maturity was attained through a relatively long series of educational opportunities, of which the last was apparently, and in his view certainly, the most decisive.

Because of this experience and earlier influences, his cast of mind was strongly historical. At Cambridge, he explained, everything after 1815 had been regarded as current affairs. His interests were much earlier and arose, it seemed, not merely from wide reading: they appeared to be imbued in him. Unsurprisingly, he had a workmanlike knowledge of the Reformation, but less so of post-Reformation history. He was much more knowledgeable about and comfortable with the medieval period and often talked as if he had been a member of the community at one of the great Yorkshire abbeys such as Rievaulx. And yet the Anglo-Saxon Church was perhaps his real spiritual home ground and he spoke about Bede and little-known saints such as Willibrord as if they were his near contemporaries. He may not have realised that he had a gift for bringing alive and integrating with his own interpretation and outlook the long-distant past, but those capable of it to a similar degree were, and are, few and far between.

If this easy familiarity with the long history of Christianity was first stimulated by his father's interests, it was inexorably deepened by his own wide reading, especially at and beyond Cambridge. It provided him with the kind of perspective not commonly found among secular clergy. Moreover, while he must have repeatedly signed the anti-modernist oath - instituted by Pius X in 1910 and not rescinded until 1967 – he had little instinctive sympathy with the kind of mind-set which thought it necessary, and still less with anyone who regarded it as desirable. Theologians may well have regarded some of his views as old-fashioned; but never as conservative, for there was no theological rigidity in him. Paradoxically, it was primarily his long historical perspective which made him keenly, indeed profoundly, interested in current developments. In due course he welcomed the deliberations and promulgations of Vatican II very warmly indeed - for many reasons but, above all, because he recognised in them an appeal to history.

There was much more to his life than an extraordinarily engaged Catholicism and a deep-seated empathy with the past. Because of his upbringing, which was quite out of the ordinary, he developed a profound knowledge of the natural world around him. When Storey was born his father, George, a keen naturalist himself, was agent of the huge Warter Priory estate of the Nunburnholme family in the East Riding of Yorkshire and the family lived at its centre in the small village of Warter, not far from Pocklington. Significantly, except for a single, week-long sojourn in York as a child, Storey's early years were spent exclusively in the countryside and, at the age of 17, Rome was the first major city that he visited. In Warter the family had a key position in the midst of a close-knit community, and were pre-eminent among a very large rural workforce, virtually all of whom could be relied on to look kindly on and share their knowledge with George's children. Spending most of his time as a child outside in the countryside, Storey developed an intimate familiarity with the landscape of the Yorkshire Wolds and its people, flora and fauna. Years later he still seemed to know, and be known by, a large proportion of its inhabitants: if, for example, one visited an agricultural show or even a local restaurant with him, he was besieged by people whose path he had previously crossed, so that either the perambulation or the meal proceeded very slowly. He drew inspiration from the Wolds area and returned there by car and then on foot for the rest of his life. He also pursued his keen interest in the natural world elsewhere, in the Lake District, Snowdonia, the Scottish Highlands and Islands, and in the many other places abroad which he visited in a long life. By conviction and in his behaviour he was a huge fan of the great outdoors and one of the earliest environmentalists. One interest, however, was pre-eminent. He had a passionate love of trees; he reared them in his own and various other gardens and then planted out tens of thousands in his native county and elsewhere; and towards the end of his life he was inclined to proclaim that 'the two most important things in life are to love – and to plant trees'.

Part of Storey's magnetism derived from his sheer human vitality. He had a fine physique, well over six feet tall and strongly built, but carrying no excess weight. Facially, he could have stepped effortlessly into the role of Sherlock Holmes, with a strong, narrow bone structure, a prominent hawk-like Roman nose, and large, piercing eyes. In his last years his eyesight deteriorated rapidly owing to macular degeneration but, that apart, he remained remarkably fit and walked for miles in any kind of terrain or type of weather until the very end. As a young man he was a talented and very active sportsman, playing rugby well, at Stonyhurst and Christ's College, and later in Middlesbrough. It was only his priesthood (and possibly promptings from his parish priest and/or his bishop) that persuaded him to decline the offer of a rugby trial for Yorkshire in the late 1940s. One tale perhaps illustrates his physical prowess better than any other. In his early eighties, just after the millennium, he was the guest of friends in the Lake District. In the morning he rose much earlier than anyone else and took his dog, Shiney, for a steep up-and-down walk of about three miles. After he had re-joined them for breakfast, the entire party set off to walk some twelve or so miles over very high ground from Hartsop, at the bottom of the Kirkstone Pass, to Howtown on the south side of Ullswater. Storey left his cap behind at an early resting point, and so had to retrace his steps for about two miles to retrieve it. Later he took a major detour into Martindale to visit a chapel before walking on to Howtown. From there everyone caught the ferry back to Glenridding and, after drinks in a pub, took cars to the cottage at Hartsop. Then, while everyone else collapsed in a heap, Storey energetically and comprehensively pruned a large buddleia in the garden. Physically, he was a phenomenon, even in old age.

He was keenly interested in current affairs and had clear views on issues of the day. As a young seminarian in Mussolini's Rome, he and a colleague narrowly escaped very serious trouble after tearing down Fascist posters. He was an enthusiastic debater at Stonyhurst, and continued this at Cambridge, and both before and during his period as Chaplain at the University of Hull. Ecumenism always came more easily to him than to most of his colleagues, clerical and lay: in his childhood and youth his had been the only Catholic family in Warter and he could recall no hostility or adverse feeling towards them because of this. For many years he was a persistent but inconspicuous supporter of the inmates of Hull prison. He became an early and active member of Amnesty International and War on Want and later was a leading and inspirational member of the Middlesbrough diocese's Justice and Peace Commission.

Despite and to a degree because of his privileged background, the foundation of these commitments was a growing belief in the need for greater social equality, together with a conviction that human relations flourished best when people treated others with respect. These attitudes developed rapidly during his first major involvement in pastoral work in post-war Middlesbrough; and were decisively confirmed during his curacy at St. Charles in Hull from 1955. Eventually his politics came to be driven by humanitarian concern and a passion for justice, both of which he regarded as fundamental to a Christian life. Such convictions were usually associated with left-wing members of religious orders, such as his friends, the Dominican priests Herbert McCabe and Lawrence Bright. Storey was among those who kept these flags flying for the secular clergy and they did not go unnoticed. On Sunday 7 October 1990 at the Annual Service of the North-Eastern Legal Circuit, he became the first Catholic cleric since the Reformation to preach in York Minster. His congregation was replete with the legally great and good – the lord lieutenant, the high sheriff, the sheriffs, the judges, and the queen's and junior counsel: the views they heard were fundamental and uncompromising.

There was one strand of Storey's manifold interests which engaged him all his life, and from which the countless numbers who sought his advice hugely benefited. This was his pre-occupation with the nature of human relationships, particularly affective relationships - love, sexual and marital relations. Over many years he actively endeavoured to discern how young people might best be inducted into these areas of life, and how sound relations might be nurtured, conducted and enriched. This was the topic of a book which he began writing towards the end of his life: but although he completed rough drafts of several chapters, increasing blindness prevented him from proceeding further. His thoughts on the subject stemmed, above all, from his personal experience of human relations. The key feature of his approach to them was that, while adhering faithfully to what was demanded of him as a celibate priest, he did not allow his celibacy or his clerical status to obscure his feelings about and with people. At a time, especially following Paul VI's encyclical *Humanae Vitae* (1968), when much Catholic ministry to lay people was shaped and largely constrained by controversy about birth control, in matters of the emotions Storey remained essentially a free spirit, a rare priestly phenomenon. In this he was deeply influenced by his adventurous and idiosyncratic reading, most especially the treatise 'On Spiritual Friendship' by St. Aelred, the twelfth-century Abbot of the Cistercian monastery at Rievaulx in north Yorkshire; and *The Art of Loving* by the German-born atheist, social philosopher and psychoanalyst, Erich Fromm. In a lifetime of wide and eclectic reading (or, latterly, being read to) these disparate and unlikely companions remained key texts whose value he never ceased to affirm. Along with the Scriptures, the influence of these two writers provided the bedrock of his conduct for the rest of his life. Aelred sowed the seed and Fromm germinated and reared it, turning his approach to life in an entirely new and constantly fulfilling direction.

In his many years as a priest, teacher and counsellor Storey encountered innumerable instances of relational problems of one kind or another. His response was positive and energetic: he regarded this as core pastoral territory and strove not merely to help those involved as they searched for solutions, but also to equip himself to be able to do so effectively. The treatment of sexual relationships in early twentieth-century Catholic seminary training was emotionally impoverished; it was also grossly distorted by a pre-occupation with sexual transgressions which derived from the juridical framework and approach of textbooks of moral theology. In forming his own views on love, sexuality and human bonding, which he came to articulate frankly and forthrightly, Storey by-passed the seminary theory and drew freely both on his reading and on a reservoir of personal and pastoral experience. His life involved a journey into an extraordinary freedom, honesty and realism about these issues, which he readily shared with others. He never lost his energy for enquiry in this sphere and never ceased to learn. While fully accepting and practising celibacy as the condition of his ministry, over the years he himself had a number of close relationships with women, including one of long standing.

He had much to offer beyond his deep wisdom about these matters. His presentation of the liturgy was customarily immaculate, with a strong emphasis on active participation by the laity. When overtaken by blindness in his later years, to the point where people wondered how he would cope saying Mass, his solution, to their delight, was to invite the entire congregation to say most of it with him. He was a compelling preacher in a quiet, undemonstrative, conversational way; and his content was largely Scripture-based long before that became common. Occasionally, if he thought attention was wandering, he would say something - 'those bastard Pharisees'- calculated to re-gather attention. His humour could also be mischievous. In retirement in November 1998 he was invited to say Mass in St. Mary's Anglican Parish Church in Beverley on the eightieth anniversary of the Armistice following the Great War. The beautiful medieval church was packed. Looking round as he came to the end of the service, Storey decided that 'we should give these stones a break after all these years', and delivered the blessing in Latin!

During the early part of his priestly career, in pre-Vatican II days, he devoted much time and energy to providing a humane interpretation of rules and regulations, doing so both informally with individuals and more formally with groups through lectures, talks and other public engagements. For the faithful then and later, both inside and outside the confessional, he was never content with the simply juridical: his spiritual encounters with them, according to widespread testimony, were imaginative and refreshing; they were also conducted in a spirit of absolute equality between the other party and himself. Following his appointment in 1962 as Catholic Chaplain at the University of Hull, Storey hugely enjoyed the regular company of younger people and was enthused by the maelstrom of cultural change during that period. But for him the most exciting development of all was the Second Vatican Council. In a process of teaching whilst sharing, he talked enthusiastically and reassuringly about it to everyone. He was emphatic that the Council was a major turning-point in his priestly life and in the life of the Church and of everyone in it. Before the Council he was often uncertain of the Church's direction; afterwards he never was.

During the late 1960s, like many others, particularly of his vintage, Storey became anxious about what he felt might be a drift towards anarchy: the disturbances at Hull University were among the most startling and widely publicised in the country, and affected Storey deeply, leading him to declare that his priority as Chaplain should have been to the University and not to the students. What also disturbed him, however, was Pope Paul VI's encyclical *Humanae Vitae.* Like many other priests, he came to regard its views as misguided: unlike most of them, he said so, not stridently but openly. His stance was that of a loyal but critical beacon of hope for a troubled laity. Subsequently, like many others, he was dismayed by what he saw as systematic attempts to ignore, retard or roll back the implementation of the decrees of Vatican II during the pontificate of John Paul II. His response was to maintain steadfastly that such efforts would be temporary in effect; that there had been many instances in the past when change had been obstructed and, therefore, slow; and that in due course there would be a flowering of the fruits of the Council.

Nor was he cast down by the loss of institutional momentum. Perhaps, indeed, he was personally re-invigorated by it. He sustained the full range of his many activities over many years until the brief but severe illness which killed him. During his last posting, to the parish of Holy Cross in Cottingham in the East Riding, he greatly enlivened an entire community; and continued to do so in the parish, St. Vincent's in Hull, where he assisted during his retirement. During these last years the emphasis of his endeavours shifted inexorably towards universal needs: for peace, equality and justice. His convictions and exhortations were always directly linked to particular problems: those with relational difficulties made more intractable by the juridical approach of powerful bodies, whether ecclesiastical or lay; the hungry in the third world; prisoners everywhere; and many others.

He won a huge following among the laity. They recognised his rock-like faith; admired his skill in articulating, defending and promoting it; and knew no other priest who laid such emphasis on the importance of their participation in everything the Church did. At the same time they knew he shared their concerns about much of what was happening in the Church and that he was unafraid of voicing them – calmly, reasonably but frankly - to whomsoever cared to listen. Above all others it was this particular combination of traits which won him a widespread following. While his superiors did not prefer him, there is no doubt that the laity did.

For many years his journey was neither smooth nor straightforward. Physically, he enjoyed good health but during many of his early and middle years he suffered from bouts of depression which he gradually learned to manage for himself. Latterly he came to enjoy, and to share, a level of peace and contentment which had often proved elusive previously; and he ended his days in calmer waters than many even aspire to. He was a remarkable, indeed amazing man who had a huge influence on those lucky enough to know him. His odyssey is traced here for the benefit of those who were and those who were not so privileged.

2: Warter Priory: the Hall.

3: Warter Priory: the view from the Hall.

CHAPTER ONE

CHILDHOOD 1919-28

Of Northumbrian stock from Rothbury, Storey's father, George Snowden Storey, was brought up in Burnley, Lancashire. The town's economy was dominated by cotton manufacturing and his solid upper-middle-class family lived at Brunshaw House on its outskirts. In 1886 at the age of eleven George was admitted to Stonyhurst, not far from Burnley, beginning in the Preparatory School at Hodder. He then passed into the upper school but stayed there only until December 1890, when he entered the Catholic junior seminary at Ushaw in Co. Durham. Either there or at Stonyhurst or both, he developed a deep interest in, and considerable knowledge of, early European history, and particularly of monasticism in the north of England. Storey derived a great deal from these special interests of his father and, as he himself testified, was much influenced by them.

Storey's paternal grandfather was a land agent and farmer, and the latest in a long line of agriculturalists who had originated in Northumberland. When George decided in 1893 that a life in orders was not for him, he returned to Burnley and was subsequently employed as an apprentice agent on the local Towneley estates. From Norman times these had belonged to the family of that name who had remained steadfast in their Catholicism since the Reformation. In 1901 they sold Towneley Hall and adjacent parkland to Burnley Corporation but still held many acres in and around the town. Storey's mother, Harriet, *nee* Folds, was also born into a well-to-do family in Burnley. Her father was a cotton manufacturer. The family lived in a prosperous part of the town at 61, Todmorden Road and in 1891 had four domestic employees. Harriet, named after her mother who was a Londoner, was the younger of two sisters and she and her sibling, Mary, were both educated at a boarding school in Kensington. The pupils there were of several nationalities: the 1901 census described the mature women at this establishment as of 'no occupation', suggesting that they were nuns and that it was a convent boarding school.

George and Harriet married in June 1909 when he was 33 and she 22. George was probably already in the post which he certainly held in 1911 - agent of the estate at Everingham Park, on the flat wetlands to the west of Beverley in east Yorkshire. This new appointment may have originated in the devolution of the Everingham property in 1908 from Baron Herries to his daughter, Lady Herries, who married Henry Fitzalan-Howard, Duke of Norfolk; and indeed it may have been his appointment as her agent which persuaded George that he and Harriet should marry. With the help of two live-in domestic staff George and Harriet set up home in a five-bedroomed house in the village of Thorpe, not far from Everingham.

For centuries Everingham Park had belonged to the Constables, a recusant family who suffered much for their Catholicism before times got easier in the later 18th century. There was (and still is) a fine Hall at Everingham, designed (1757-64) by John Carr, the most celebrated of Yorkshire architects. The adjacent Italianate church of SS. Mary and Everilda, built in 1829 (almost certainly from architectural plans obtained from Italy), was the first Catholic chapel to be opened after the Emancipation Act - a small basilica, set incongruously in the east Yorkshire countryside. Following the earlier failure of the Constables in the male line, the estate had passed by marriage to the Haggerstons of Haggerston in Northumberland; then to the Herries family; and finally to the Norfolks, thereby never departing from Catholic ownership. It was an impressive, indeed prestigious appointment for George Storey; and others were to follow.

Storey himself frequently talked about the next stage in his father's career, which came in 1915, four years before his own birth. During the First World War mechanised transport became increasingly important. From the start, however, there continued to be a huge demand for horses, particularly from the military. It was George Storey's responsibility on behalf of the government to gather these animals from all over the north of England and train them before they were sent to destinations at home and abroad. In view of the national prominence of the Norfolks, this post may have been held alongside that at Everingham. The greater likelihood, however, is that its duties were full-time; and that, while his appointment owed much to the Norfolks' support, in taking it George was obliged to leave their employ. This seems to be confirmed by the fact that the post was based in York, and that in 1916 one of Storey's older brothers, Peter, was born in Acomb, a suburb of the city.

The summit of George Storey's career came immediately after the war, with his appointment as agent of the Nunburnholme family's estate in the East Riding. The Warter Priory estate, re-named after a local but dissolved house of Augustinian canons, was among the largest and grandest of Yorkshire's landed prop-erties. It lay next to the small village of Warter near Pocklington, had a massive mansion at its centre, and was then presided over by the formidable Lady Nunburnholme, a great-niece of the 1st Duke of Wellington. She was the widow (since 1907) of Charles Wilson, the Hull magnate who, with his brother, had greatly ex-panded the Wilson Shipping Line and served as Liberal M.P. for Hull (1874-1905) before being raised to the peerage as Lord Nun-burnholme in 1906. The property had for long been owned by the Penningtons, Lords Muncaster; and it was they who during

4: Storey as a child (2nd from left) with (from left) Aidan, Agatha, Peter & Gerard.

the Victorian period had re-named and extended Warter Hall, hitherto a modest country house, by re-fronting it and creating corner towers. The Penningtons sold the house and estate to Charles Wilson in 1878. He soon embarked on extensive alterations and additions, including a great hall, a three-storey clock tower over the entrance, and a grand marble staircase. When he had finished, the house had nearly 100 bedrooms and was the focal point of an estate of just under 30,000 acres, most of which was prime agricultural land. As agent George Storey led an estate workforce of around 1,000 people.

He was also head of a growing family. They lived in a house, the 'Old Vicarage', in the centre of Warter. The eldest child, George Gerard (usually known as Gerard) was born in 1911. John followed in 1913, and Agatha in 1914. There were three more sons, firstly Peter, born in 1916, then Aidan, and finally Anthony

Joseph. Not long after his father had taken up his new appointment, Storey was born at home in Warter on 6 March 1919. His birth was registered on the following day and he was baptised in the church of SS. Mary and Joseph in Pocklington on the 13 March.

Great estates, a major feature of English landownership for generations, had steadily declined in the face of the agricultural challenges of the later 19th century, particularly competition from international trade. This process was intensified by the introduction of death duties in the 1890s and their elaboration during the early 1900s; and then by very heavy mortality among the officer class during the Great War, which disrupted and often obliterated lines of inheritance. In the nature and scale of its operations during Storey's early years the Warter Priory estate was one of the last of its kind. Every acre of this vast property, and indeed every single building on it, belonged to the Nunburnholmes. For those who lived and worked there, relations were strictly hierarchical and Lady Nun, as she was known, presided at their apex. In his early years Storey was instructed that, if he encountered her, he was not to block his face: he had to raise his cap - on the right side if she passed to his left, and on the left side if she passed to his right. Similar salutes had to be paid to the farmers, most of whom, though they were tenants, were substantial and prosperous people; and to the leading estate employees, such as the head gamekeeper and the head woodman. On the other hand, lesser mortals such as labourers, ploughboys and the like were expected to salute Storey and his brothers and sisters. This was the kind of heavy, inequitable formality with which afterwards he had no patience.

Up at the big house, in addition to lots more etiquette, there were many features that a boy was likely to find attractive or impressive: the beautiful furniture in the Queen Anne, the French and the Italian suites and in the huge dining room; the organ in the great hall; and above all perhaps the trophies of lions' and elephants' heads brought back from Africa. The Priory was the only property in the village with electric light, powered by a generator and supported by innumerable glass batteries distributed around the house. This facility was managed by a man named Tasker, who doubled up as chauffeur of the family's Daimler. The big house also had running water, upstairs as well as downstairs. This was achieved through use of a Victorian invention, a Blake's Hydram, which was supplied from a water tower. So 'old Noble', the plumber, was another key employee. A third was Wright, the head groom, who looked after the many horses and their tackle. A vivid memory was of Wright's mirth when, as a nine or ten-year-old, Storey tried his first cigarette and felt utterly sick. The key roles played by Tasker, Noble and Wright were signified by the fact that, along with the local vicar, they all lived in the same row of houses as Storey's family in Warter, and he got to know each of them extremely well

Among Storey's memories of Warter was the spontaneous care of the less advantaged villagers: for example, John Patrick, the estate mole catcher who worked alongside the gamekeepers.

The community looked after him….we would try to keep him going. He was a bit dopey (at least of very limited intelligence) and he used to live by killing his moles and selling the velvet to make waistcoats. And then there was another chap walking round the village: he was probably a Down's syndrome young man, but we used to call him the Cuckoo. I think we always thought that anyone with a mental defect, who wasn't bad enough to go into a mental institution but who were [sic] permanently or chronically ill, had been rendered so by being born on the wrong side of the sheets or something. And so that was an unkind way but we were always very friendly with the Cuckoo, a simple lad.

Later, when chaplain at St. Luke's Mental Hospital in Middlesbrough, an influential experience during his early curacies, Storey was acutely embarrassed by these attitudes.

Large numbers of fashionable people descended on Warter Priory, particularly at weekends. House parties were a feature of life in high society during the inter-war period. At Warter Lady Nun was not just a generous hostess in the spring and summer (she also had a summer residence at Cottingham): her main property had a reputation (which it retains) as an excellent shooting estate in the autumn and winter. It was a key part of George Storey's responsibilities to ensure that shooting parties were successful; and in this he was assisted by Tom England, the head gamekeeper, who had six to eight other keepers working under him, housed at salient points throughout the estate. They tended the pheasants, particularly during the breeding season, controlled a range of vermin, and also at night time repelled would-be poachers from the industrial West Riding. Foxes were culled through regular hunts. Guests, anxious to behave appropriately, invariably participated in full hunting dress, but Storey and his siblings and the local lads on their cobs and ponies were excused this. He always maintained that, as far as they were concerned, killing foxes was not the focal point of hunting: the hectic ride was the chief thrill, and the competition to get across dykes and hedges and first into a field. His father ensured that there were responsibilities as well as fun, instructing him always to look out for the senior politician (later Foreign Secretary in Neville Chamberlain's government), Lord Halifax, who owned an estate centred on Garrowby on the edge of the Wolds, and had only one arm; and to be ready to open a gate for him so that Halifax could avoid waiting for somebody else to do so and also stay in his saddle.

Core business, however, was less concerned with leisure than with the inexorable routine of the farming year. The family lived in a very distinctive agricultural landscape. With the Vale of Pickering to the north and the Humber to the south, flat wetlands to the west and the North Sea to the east, the Wolds were high, rounded chalk hills, intersected by deep valleys, many of which were dry. From the hills there were vistas in every direction, but from the valleys one could see nothing except the adjacent hillsides. The region was not cut off, but the Wolds looked and felt apart from what lay around them.

The farming system was also distinctive. Until pioneering work in the 18th century the Wolds had been largely uncultivated for centuries. Later, cereals became the dominant crop and the estate had twenty or so farms, one of which, as was customary, was run by George Storey and his family, though as agent George had oversight of all of them. The scale of the operations involved in running such a huge estate greatly impressed the agent's youngest son. In a 100-acre field, for example, he once saw eight teams of horses ploughing, harrowing, rolling and sowing; and at harvest time six to eight binders, with dozens of men stooking. It was then the turn of the traction engine and the thrashing machine to visit the farms in turn.

As the stacks were being lowered and the corn was going through the machine, rats started pouring out from the bottom of the stacks and the machines would stop and everyone would go dashing around beating up rats, trying to catch them as they were going up gutters, and you had to be careful they didn't run up your trouser leg….Those farms that were left till late on the schedule were often really badly infested with rats by the time the traction engine came round to them.

As soon as the cereals were off the land sheep were overwintered on green crops: in Storey's time, through his father's connections, the animals were brought down in huge wagons from Rothbury. In autumn too Irish cattle were stall-fed on clover, turnips and kale before being slaughtered in the spring. The need for access to water posed particular problems on the chalky Wolds. In Warter the main spring came out near the church. Huge horse-drawn water carts filled up there and took water to farms on the higher ground to supplement the little that could be got from the carefully constructed dew ponds. Storey registered all this year on year as a child, building up a deep understanding of farming and the agricultural year, and an empathy with those who lived that life and with the countryside where they worked.

There was much else to witness on a busy great estate. There were extensive woods, many of them wind breaks, to be kept in good fettle. The head woodman managed a gang of men who worked with shire horses, pulling out trees and dragging them on derricks down to the sawmill, which was rarely idle. In the middle of the village was the blacksmith's forge, always a focus of activity. It was the blacksmith's job to keep the horses well shod and to repair ploughs and other implements. He could be relied on to mend children's hoops and the runners on their toboggans, as well as the skates used by nearly everyone on the frozen village ponds in winter.

The internal combustion engine made its way into the East Riding countryside relatively slowly and throughout Storey's childhood the chief means of transport for those who could afford it was on horseback. His father was an excellent horseman and, using a little yellow-coloured Icelandic pony called 'Dickie', made sure that all his children could ride at an early age. Soon after Storey learned to ride, and as his older brothers left home, he joined the daily routine of exercising the horses used by his father and the family:

riding for miles on the roads over the Wolds. They weren't tarmacked….[so] we'd often ride on the verges; and there would be dykes letting the water off and they'd puddle so we'd jump the ditches and we learnt elementary horsemanship from that. And grooming them and clipping them and taking care of them was very major in our lives.

This was not much fun on cold winter mornings, but it took him round the locality regularly and made him thoroughly familiar with everything going on there. In the course of a year he rode over every hill and through every valley in the western Wolds. He recalled occasions when his family travelled on horseback as far as the east coast. His knowledge of rural life in the East Riding was profound and much of it was gained while riding.

Horses were also at the root of his love of personal freedom. His brother, John, who outlived him, unwittingly threw light on this in conversation shortly before his own death. After leaving school in the 1930s, he was employed in a solicitor's office in Whitefriargate in the centre of Hull and lived in digs in the city. Having enjoyed the same freedom to ride all over the Wolds, he hated urban life, particularly dull office work, and determined to break free. Seeing a poster offering opportunities in the police service in Palestine, he applied, was successful and spent his career keeping order, successively in Palestine, British Honduras, Brunei and Sarawak. On retirement he and his family moved to Western Australia. Anyone who knew Storey well will testify that, while willing to give endless time, night or day, to those in need, as soon as he felt that someone was trying to manage or corral him, he too would break free. Exercising the horses was a job that had to be done: but for him it was also a deeply influential experience. Like John, the mobile freedom it gave him as a child marked him for life. The impact of his youthful experience on the Wolds went even further: in 1966 'I find I need the sheer freedom of the hills and the wild and the wet in order to find peace'.

Storey had a good relationship with John: it was from him

that he got his first sex education, which was confined to the mechanics. Later, both his sisters had a warm and frank relationship with Storey, no doubt rooted in earlier experiences. He recalled feeling close to his brothers and sisters: but he also remembered occasionally being 'fearful' of them and, in particular, of 'being very seriously bullied by my eldest brother', Gerard. The accusation from Gerard that most upset Storey was that he was not much good at the things most country kids did. He recalled stealing Gerard's airgun in retaliation and walking up a hedgerow.

> We had seen a blackbird sitting on its nest. I was very ashamed....I shot it just to prove that I could shoot, I could kill. I came away feeling shame and never told anybody about this. It was so destructive. I was being damaged. It was a point of change.

These memories formed part of his reflections in later life on his first experience of relationships. He did not feel that he had been greatly damaged by being bullied and ultimately was more concerned about the bully. The episode was the precursor of related experiences during his schooldays. While he had an enjoyable, almost idyllic, childhood, some clouds crossed his sky.

As he grew up Storey became increasingly conscious of change. The road from Pocklington to Warter, hitherto chalk-based, was tarmacadamed. The first binder arrived to replace the traditional hay-reaper. He was present during the first attempt – in Mrs. Bean's shop – to bring radio to the village via a 'great square box loaded up with wires all over the place', only for efforts to be defeated by a sudden and very violent thunderstorm. The extension of the franchise to women in 1928 also registered with him, though even more startling, at least to his mother, was the decision of the village general practitioner, Dr. Fair, to appoint a female assistant doctor. Amidst such developments, Storey's childhood was passed in a large community and stable environment where all were involved in some way in the same enterprise; and where the guiding hand, especially in times of difficulty, was that of his father.

Storey was away at preparatory school when Lady Nun died in 1932, but he returned for the funeral and left a vivid account:

> Lady Nun's funeral was tremendous. All the lords and ladies in the area seemed to be attending it. And the wagon with four great black horses – a Wolds wagon – carried the coffin from the Priory right down the village to the cemetery in the village church. After the lords and ladies came the butler and the footman, and the maids, and the head gardener and the gardeners, and then the game keepers, and then the woodmen and the farmers. It was a huge procession, all really properly dressed, and we as kids were outside it up a little lane. And when they went past we had in our care one of our dogs, a little white West Highland terrier. And it spied my Dad in the procession amongst the estate staff and left us and rushed to him. So we giggled away as this very solemn procession went round the village with little Scottie....trotting along beside my dad.

It was the end of an era in Warter.

George had a challenging job and was exceedingly busy. Storey was the youngest of six children until Patience was born in 1926. Inevitably, he saw little of his father and at this stage of his life was not close to him. Indeed, he got to know his father really well only after ordination in 1943, during the few years before George's death in 1947. Moreover, in his uncompleted memoir Storey had little to say about his mother, despite undertaking to discuss her influence before finishing it. He never got round to doing so, eventually judging the memoir to be of poor quality; in any case, increasing blindness prevented his return to it. In correspondence in May 2005, however, he had this to say about his mother's care during his childhood. 'I realise I have hardly spoken of my Mum, who literally was my life and lifeline.' She 'was a wonderful Catholic lady'. This tribute was heartfelt because he came under his mother's direct, daily influence for far longer than most children, leaving for school at Freshfield only in September 1928 when he was nine-and-a-half years old. Harriet not only taught him to read and write: she also introduced him to more than the rudiments of several subjects; and it was she who nurtured him in the Catholic faith, instilling in him a particular devotion to Christ's mother, Mary.

This extended domestic childhood may shed some light on the sort of young Catholic Storey grew up to be: utterly loyal to his heritage and the Church, persistently upbeat about his faith and quick to defend it, and yet questioning anything that occurred to him. While many contemporary Catholics would have had positive comments to make about their education in Catholic primary schools, in retrospect they would also have highlighted negative features, in particular the emphasis on how easy it was to transgress and the dangerous spiritual consequences of doing so. The religious pedagogy of the day too easily encouraged individuals to feel guilt-ridden from their earliest years. Storey certainly felt 'plagued' by guilt in his youth, 'taught it', he maintained, 'by our childhood preparation for and practice of confession', which was perhaps one reason why, as a priest, he was such a sympathetic and constructive confessor. However, he appears not to have been deeply infected by feelings of guilt and, as he reached maturity, to have had very little negativity to discard. The unusual nature of his own early education led to the development of a more positive attitude: one which was seldom shared by many of his Catholic contemporaries.

One of his other characteristics may also have been his

mother's legacy, though it was no doubt also fashioned by later pastoral experience. In his thinking about personal relations Storey seemed never to have the slightest difficulty in judging situations from the female point of view. He was occasionally accused of being overtly pro-woman. He did not resent this accusation, regarding his stance as a necessary corrective to conventional male attitudes. In this respect, perhaps above all others, his approach was radically different from that of his brother, Peter, who also became a priest. Throughout his life Fr. Peter Storey's attitude towards women was to have as little to do with them as possible, so much so that it would not be unfair to describe him as a mysoginist. On this issue the two men were poles apart, partly perhaps because one of them had a longer and closer relationship with their mother than the other.

The Storeys were the only Catholic family on the Warter estate. Later, knowing that others had experienced a different reaction to their beliefs, he went out of his way to stress that no difficulty had arisen because of this isolation. They lived next door to the vicar, the Revd. Atkinson, and the children of both families played together. The better-off, including the farmers, attended the Anglican parish church of St. James in Warter; most of the rest went to the village's little Methodist chapel; and the Storeys travelled, 'either in the pony trap or later on in a grotty old Ford', to the Catholic church of SS. Mary and Joseph in Pocklington. Under a recusant family, the Dolmans, a Catholic community had existed there from at least 1790. A tiny chapel had been built in 1807, near the market place in the centre of the town, and in 1862-63 this was replaced by a new Gothic building on the same site. Eventually the Storeys filled an entire bench in the church, with another country family, the Coopers, farmers from Huggate, filling the one behind them. In a local population of between 3,000 and 4,000, the number of Catholics attending the church fluctuated around 150.

Then and for long afterwards Catholics were required to

send their children to Catholic schools if at all possible. There was no Catholic school in the Wolds area, though a tiny one-teacher school was attached to the parish in Pocklington. However, all George and Harriet's children went to private Catholic boarding schools, the boys to Bishop's Court Preparatory School at Freshfield in Lancashire, and the girls to a boarding school run by the Sisters of the Sacred Heart at Beechwood Hall, near Tunbridge Wells in Sussex. No doubt their parents wished their children to benefit from a thoroughly sound Catholic education, as indeed they had done. But also, according to Storey, 'that snobbish thing was very much there....we shouldn't be mixing with the village children because we were part of the estate management'. Looking back, he 'regretted very much not being at one with the village children except for games and sport'. Leaving Warter brought about a major change in his way of life.

CHAPTER TWO

SCHOOLDAYS 1928-36

On the coast between Liverpool and Southport, Freshfield lay north of Formby on Merseyside. Ever since the railway age it has been regarded as a desirable place to live. The Liverpool, Crosby and Southport section of the London, Midland and Scottish railway opened in 1848; and the place-name Freshfield was chosen for the station established there in 1854, after Thomas Fresh, the local landowner, who was also Liverpool's Inspector of Nuisances. Together with William Duncan, the U.K.'s first Medical Officer of Health, and James Newlands, Borough Engineer, he was one of the trio of public officials celebrated for their contribution to the health and welfare of the population of Merseyside during Victoria's reign.

Urban growth in northern England was rapid during the 19th century. It promoted residential development in rural areas close to major cities, and was greatly facilitated by the growth of railways. Liverpool's wealthier merchants and businessmen preferred to live in the countryside and soon their large houses generated significant demand for both domestic and outdoor staff. Although the surrounding area remained primarily a farming community, the population of the Formby district grew from the time the railway station opened, and reached some 7,000 by 1940. When Storey arrived Freshfield was prosperous, though much quieter and less developed than it is today.

A boys' preparatory college had been founded in Freshfield in 1892 as an independent Roman Catholic school by a redoubtable woman, Miss Emma Gosford. With her sister she

5: Bishop's Court at Freshfield.

had previously run a successful day school for girls in Liverpool. Her new school for boys was so successful and grew so rapidly that the property at Bishop's Court was purchased in 1894 and greatly enlarged two years later. A link with Stonyhurst was soon forged and one of the first pupils to proceed from one school to the other, in 1896, was the future, celebrated Jesuit, Fr. Martin D'Arcy. Miss Gosford soldiered on till retirement in 1920 and in 1921 her half-century of educational endeavour in Merseyside was rewarded with the Papal Diploma and Cross 'Pro Ecclesia et Pontifice'. In 1924 the school moved from Victoria Lane in Freshfield to a more promising site in Wrigley's Lane, previously the home of a wealthy family of that name. When Storey arrived there in the autumn of 1928 the establishment was run by two formidable ladies. The Principal, who had succeeded Emma Gosford, was Miss Grace Trevor, and Mrs. M.A. Barham-Robins was her deputy. According to Storey, one was a graduate of Cambridge and the other of Oxford, and they chose to be colour-coded with one customarily dressed in red and the other in blue.

Because of its well-to-do residential character, with larger properties periodically coming on the market, Freshfield was well supplied with churches, medical facilities, nursing homes, and schools. A substantial proportion of the population were Catholics and the largest congregation of any denomination was at the church of Our Lady of Compassion in nearby Formby. In 1884 the Mill Hill Missionary Fathers had opened an establishment in Freshfield which eventually became St. Peter's College. By the 1920s it housed a junior seminary and a novitiate. In addition to several other schools, there were two preparatory schools for boys: Bishop's Court, and Holmwood in nearby College Avenue, which also had a junior department. Bishop Court's stated aim was to prepare its pupils 'for the Catholic Public Schools'. It took boys from 7 to 14 years old on what were described as 'moderate terms'.

The local landscape could scarcely have been less like the one Storey left behind in east Yorkshire. It was flat with virtually no horizon and was flanked to the west by sand dunes running down to the sea. Then, as now, the area was a noted habitat for both red squirrels and natterjack toads. Storey remembered walks 'down to the beach to see the red squirrels in the trees and the dunes. It was lovely'. He had particularly 'good fun….learning to swim'. The most striking comment he made about Bishop's Court, however, was critical: friendships at the school were close; and he ascribed this chiefly to the fact that 'the authority over us was very powerful'.

It was both powerful and extremely strict. Boys were not allowed to speak in the dormitories and developed their own sign language.

There was loads of physical punishment. I remember

kneeling with a broken plate during the whole length of a meal to show I was sorry for having dropped the damn plate, holding it up in the air. And I remember staying hours behind when I hadn't finished the porridge. I had to sit there the whole morning and I wasn't allowed out of the breakfast room until I'd finished it. Lots of other boys had physical punishment.

This sort of regime was almost calculated to provoke a strong reaction from someone, but when it came it was fiercer than anyone could have imagined. One pupil, Anthony Michael Dominic George, was a friend of Storey and a year ahead of him - he always remembered the name because the initials were identical to those of the Jesuit motto, *Ad Majorem Dei Gloriam,* so prominently displayed later at Stonyhurst. George tried to burn the place down, and with it the Principal and her Deputy who lived on the top floor; and very nearly succeeded. The fire brigade quelled the blaze, but it took considerable time to identify who was responsible. Eventually the whole school was ordered out on parade and Mr. Vincent Bullen, Drill Master (P.E. teacher) at Bishop's Court for 48 years, asked each pupil in turn, face to face, whether he was the culprit. Storey's negative response, he recalled with deep resentment, was followed by the comment: 'too scatter-brained'. Under this procedure George found it impossible to maintain his innocence - Bullen 'just knew the eyes' - confessed to the police, and was expelled. Later, re-united with Storey at Stonyhurst, they reminisced happily about the incident.

Among Storey's other memories of Bishop's Court was his resentment at being criticised 'for always writing essays about my dog', a terrier called 'Cinders' to which he was very attached. There was also the letter he received from his father telling him that Dickie, the little Icelandic pony on which he had learned to ride, had 'gone the way of all flesh'. This turn of phrase had to be explained to him, whereupon he wept: it was his first experience of the death of an animal he loved. On another occasion he was greatly excited by sight of the enormous Graf Zeppelin flying over Liverpool. Later at Warter, while on holiday from school, he went down to the huge hangar at Howden, where the R100 had been built, to view the airship, 'climbing all over it'; and in July 1930 he saw it launched from Howden on its successful trans-Atlantic journey to Canada.

After returning to Freshfield later that year he prepared for the sacrament of Confirmation, which he received in November 1930 from the Archbishop of Liverpool, in the church of Our Lady of Compassion in Formby. Almost predictably for someone whose love of nature was by then well established, Storey took the confirmation name of Francis. It was about this time that he conceived a wish to go on pilgrimage to Assisi, which he was able to fulfil many years later. This period at Bishop's Court was also 'the first time I got a moral awareness of war and the evil of war and the horrors of it, and the heroism of the men who had to put up with it'. This was an attitude which was to last a lifetime. Its instigator was Vincent Bullen, the Drill Master who had disparaged Storey during the parade after the fire. He had been a sergeant-major on the Somme and, much to Storey's discomfiture, regaled the boys with graphic descriptions of his wartime experiences. Even at that early age, Storey felt that this was inappropriate behaviour for someone who had charge of young boys.

A more personal experience at Bishop's Court gave him pause for thought for many years afterwards. He recalled telling a fellow pupil, Paul William, that he wanted him to be his special friend. Although not an uncommon feeling among young boys, Storey never fully understand this need for an exclusive friendship. Subsequently still more troubling, especially in view of his own earlier bullying by his older brother, Gerard, was the memory of his bullying William when they spent some vacation time together at Warter. 'I quite suddenly found myself teasing, and actually bullying and making him cry'.

> It didn't last, and I don't think it destroyed our friendship, though I later grew away from it….Somehow, I believe, this may be a part of growing into self-awareness and in biblical terms the meaning of pride and self-asserting and power called original sin. It is the fall of every man.

This was not his first experience of bullying; nor was it to be his last.

Storey's life at Bishop's Court was probably softened somewhat by the presence of older brothers. Three of them preceded him there but by the time Storey arrived, Gerard, the eldest, had left the school: so the newest of them was known as Storey 3. He looked back on the school with distinctly mixed feelings.

> It was pretty awful but we did learn….[The two ladies] were very frightening people and they certainly got us through exams. Most of the boys managed to go to other colleges without too much trouble. Certainly, this was a cramming place. But it wasn't altogether with loads of love.

It got him to where both he and his parents wanted him to be.

As for the future, there was a still more significant episode at Bishop's Court when Storey had his first intimation that he was being called to the priesthood. It came out of the blue and he did not welcome it. The Mill Hill Missionary Fathers at St. Peter's College often supplied a priest to say Mass at Bishop's Court and it was while Storey was serving as an altar boy that the episode took place.

> I remember once in a procession there one of the Fathers was just home from Africa. And when he was giving the

blessing during the service - I was a little altar boy - I remember somehow his eyes pierced right into me and I realised I somehow was being told I had to become a priest. We were always being told we ought to pray for vocations to the priesthood and religious life and I hadn't the slightest interest in it. It wasn't for me, but somehow I felt, oh what the hell as though I'd been caught, and it bugged me. Neither my father nor my mother thought that I had a vocation; it was very questionable and so it went to the back of my mind.

But it never left his mind. However much he may have wished that it had not happened, this was an unforgettable, and key, experience.

Storey took Bishop's Court in his stride but was not fond of the place. Peter (though not the other two brothers at Bishop's Court) preceded him to Stonyhurst, but left for the junior seminary at Ushaw a year before Storey arrived. Admitted in 1932 (with at least one other boy from Bishop's Court), Storey greatly enjoyed Stonyhurst and found it a breath of fresh air after his prep school. The College had a major influence on his outlook, particularly towards his faith.

Bishop's Court was a young institution which advertised itself as preparing pupils for 'the Catholic Public Schools'. Stonyhurst, was one such and an ancient establishment, having been founded in 1593 by the English Jesuit exile, Fr. Robert Persons, at St. Omer in what was then the Spanish Netherlands. Its purpose was to provide a Catholic education for young Englishmen, which in penal times was strictly forbidden to them in their own country. Adverse circumstances forced the College to move to Bruges in 1762, and to Liege in 1773. Subsequently, a former pupil, Thomas Weld, inherited premises and land at Stonyhurst previously owned by the Catholic Shireburne family. It was his donation of this property to the Jesuits which enabled the College, with a mere dozen pupils, to migrate to north Lancashire in 1794.

The new century witnessed profound changes to the College. It acquired further property and eventually owned almost 4,000 acres. A Preparatory School was established in 1807, and a Novitiate for aspirants to the Society of Jesus in 1828. By mid-century Stonyhurst was the organisational hub of the English Jesuits. From the late 1870s the central premises were substantially refurbished and greatly extended, bringing them to the state and shape that Storey later enjoyed. These developments enhanced the quality of the College's accommodation, enabling it to compete effectively with its peers (including other Jesuit schools) in the face of growing demand from the middle classes for private education. By the turn of the century Stonyhurst was a, perhaps *the,* leading Catholic public school. In addition to an excellent academic record, the College was permeated by religious practice and Ignatian spirituality and its system produced 'a simplicity of moral outlook and an acceptance of common duty', precisely what parents were looking for.

Beyond the Great War this pre-eminence was not sustained. There was fierce competition from other Jesuit schools and from Benedictine establishments at Downside and Ampleforth. Internally, while annual enrolments grew to over 300, the move of the seminary in 1926 to Heythrop in Oxfordshire brought a sharp decline in Jesuit numbers at Stonyhurst, from 134 in 1924 to 47 a decade later. This adversely affected the quality of teaching, especially as extra-curricular activities were simultaneously expanded in the face of competition from elsewhere. However, while the College faced stiff challenges, it remained a fine school and Storey enjoyed himself and took full advantage of his opportunity.

Throughout Storey's time the College was led by Fr. Edward O'Connor, among its most successful Rectors and the only one to serve two full terms in the position. Earlier a multi-talented student - an Oxford double-First in Maths, an outstanding musician and a fine athlete – Fr. O'Connor's first term as Rector, 1916-24, was 'epoch-making'. His contribution as a builder and developer (most notably the installation of a self-contained College power station, which generated electricity but was also linked to the heating system) was surpassed only by Fr. Purbrick who had created the south-east front during the 19th century. Fr. O' Connor then became Choirmaster and Director of Stonyhurst's Observatory. His second term as Rector, 1932-38, saw further significant building developments, including new swimming facilities and playing fields. These endeavours were complemented by those of a very different character, Fr. Ernest Clark, a former pupil, who was 'First Prefect' from 1931, responsible for the routine operation of the College. Clark had no claim to academic distinction but put his stamp firmly on everyday life. He was particularly kind to new students and his response to transgressions was imaginative: it was compulsory for students to attend morning Mass, but anyone missing it was required to compose a sonnet. Something which Storey would have appreciated - before the rapid growth of motorised transport Stonyhurst remained very isolated - was Clark's willingness to allow students, particularly senior ones, to roam over the estate and surrounding countryside. Moreover, besides being renowned for his Marian devotion and his twice-daily availability in the confessional, the First Prefect was very keen on both rugby and cricket, two of Storey's favourite sports.

A variety of other talented individuals worked alongside these two men. Fr. George Walkerley was 'a real boy's man: very strong character, straight and honest gaze, lantern jaw, fine physique [and] good boxer'. Fr. John Firth, once a pupil at Stonyhurst, returned as a scholastic (a Jesuit not yet ordained) while Storey was there. He was a good rugby player and a keen debater. Another scholastic, Christopher John Devlin, was on the staff when Storey arrived. He was regarded as 'perhaps the most gifted [Jesuit] of his generation in the English province', and later produced well-regarded books on the poet and martyr, Robert Southwell, and on Gerard Manley Hopkins. Fr. Henry Macklin, who taught Maths at Stonyhurst for decades, was another avid sportsman, particularly fond of rugby and cricket. He was also someone who regularly walked for miles across the north Lancashire countryside, as Storey did in various parts of Britain throughout his life. Percy Haddock and Christopher Hollis were among the steadily growing number of lay masters. Haddock spent 48 years teaching Chemistry and Maths at Stonyhurst, his only appointment, and was a particularly fine cricketer. Hollis, a recent convert and Oxford graduate, taught Storey History at Stonyhurst and later kept in touch with him. Although the staff were fewer in number than had once been the case, they were a talented group with strong personalities and much to offer. There was a firm commitment: to intellectual endeavour; to extra-curricular activities, especially sport; and to the Catholic faith.

The Jesuits had established education as their primary ministry from the time of their foundation in the mid-16th century. They sought to educate the whole person; and unlike some religious orders founded later, they saw no conflict between high intellectual attainment and personal spiritual development. This was at the root of one of Storey's most striking characteristics – his relentless quest to get to the bottom of things, in particular matters relating to his faith. Even on his death bed he was to admit being puzzled by the doctrine of the Trinity and wished he fully understood it.

His academic record at Stonyhurst was very impressive. In any form an 'Imperator' was the leading prize awarded for excellent work. Admitted to Upper Rudiments I in September 1932, a level which testified to the high regard in which he was

6: Stonyhurst: Campion Under 14 Rugby XV
(Storey on the far right).

held as an entrant, he won the 'Imperator' for his compositions and general schoolwork during his very first term. He was immediately moved up to Lower Grammar I where he was awarded the 'Imperator' for the next term from January 1933. There was nothing 'scatter-brained' about this performance. Academically, he stood out from the start.

Among the College's efforts to improve its educational record was the presentation of many more candidates for public examinations: whereas, for instance, only two pupils had taken the Oxford & Cambridge Higher School Certificate in 1920, 30 did so in 1930. Storey wasted no time in confronting this hurdle. He passed his Lower School Certificate in 1933 at the end of his first year, achieving a first class in Additional Maths, and second classes in Latin, Greek, French, English and Arithmetic. A year later, aged only 15 years and 3 months, he gained his Higher School Certificate, passing with credit in six subjects – English,

History, Latin, Greek, French (written and oral) and Elementary Mathematics. By any standards this was a fine performance. It was very rare indeed for a Stonyhurst pupil to gain a Higher Certificate at such a young age and after only two years at the College.

Taking the College's motto to heart (*Quant je puis*/As well as I possibly can), Storey pursued a variety of extra-curricular activities, of which perhaps the most important – at least in terms of his enjoyment and commitment of time – was rugby. Until shortly after the Great War soccer had been the chief winter sport at Stonyhurst. The change to rugby in 1921-22, instituted by Fr. O'Connor, was motivated by the need to remain competitive with other public schools. Previously, external competitive games of rugby had been few and against club sides. By the late 1930s the Stonyhurst First XV was playing around 20 away fixtures a year against other schools. This also motivated another change in 1922, one which had significant implications for sport – the division of the College into the four Lines (not Houses) of Campion, Shireburne, St. Omers and Weld. Storey was a member of Campion.

He played home matches for Campion throughout his Stonyhurst career. He was also picked for the College Under Fourteen team during his first year. During his second he played for the Campion 2nd XV; and early in the following year he became a member of the College 2nd XV. During October in his final year the 2nd XV defeated Oldham Academy 11-8, and a fortnight later, 'in wind and driving rain', they won 39-0 against the 2nd XV of Giggleswick Grammar School. He was awarded his 2nd XV colours in November. Team photographs suggest that Storey was physically a late developer and, in any case, he was young for his year group: it took time for his subsequently imposing physique to develop. He played only a modest part in

7: Stonyhurst: the 2nd XV, 1935-36
(Storey front row, 2nd from left).

the process whereby over more than two decades rugby was thoroughly established as the main winter sport at Stonyhurst. College teams became more regularly successful soon after his time. Yet among his age-group he was an able player and his love of the sport lasted.

Cricket was played during the short summer period down to early July. Inevitably, it was less elaborately organised than rugby, at least at the level at which Storey played, with most matches being against teams (including a staff team) gathered together by Old Boys. In the summer of 1935 he was picked for the College 3rd XI, at once producing his best-ever performance when, in a game against the estate staff and batting at first wicket down, he scored 20 runs – the second-highest for his team, who nevertheless lost. He continued to play for the 3rd XI until he left Stonyhurst, but neither he nor the team covered themselves in glory. While he was keen on cricket, he was not blessed with as much natural ability as he had at rugby

He was considerably more successful as a runner, particu-

8: Stonyhurst: Sports Team 1936
(Storey back row, far right).

larly over the longer distances, putting in a notable performance during his first year. On 14 April 1933 70 pupils competed over a distance of almost five miles. Despite having played rugby and scored a try for Campion on the previous day, Storey came eighth overall and was second home for his Line. Later, at the College Sports Day in the summer, he came third in the steeplechase. Curiously, there is no record of his running in session 1933-34, but in a cross-country run on 19 April 1935 he was sixth in the second set to come in and the first Campion man home. Just before Easter in the following year he came eighth in a 40-strong field for a cross-country run and was the second home for Campion. Afterwards he was chosen as part of a College Athletics team to compete against Rossall School. At the College Sports Day he came second in a heat for the mile and before he left Stonyhurst he was awarded his colours for Athletics.

Nothing competed with sport as an extra-curricular activity. Yet these years saw the beginning of something else which he came to enjoy greatly. Most of those who encountered Storey in

43

his middle years, as University Chaplain for example, knew of his penchant for debating. Long before he became Chaplain he accepted invitations to speak in the University Debates Union, and most of his many friends among non-Catholic students first encountered him there. Unless the activity featured at Bishop's Court, which seems unlikely, he had his first experience of this verbal jousting at Stonyhurst.

His initial appearance as a listed speaker came in December 1934 when he opposed the motion: 'In the opinion of this House blood sports are to be deplored'. Against the background of his life at Warter, he could scarcely have found a better topic on which to make a maiden speech. Speaking vividly from experience, he argued that it was essential to rid farmland of vermin, so why not 'make a pleasure of it?' This was done most effectively with dogs. Yet you had to employ a number of them, not just one or two, and a pack could be controlled only by a huntsman, who had to have colleagues, which was why the sport had evolved in its current form. Drag-hunts, where hounds simply followed an artificial scent laid down in advance, left him 'cold'. There was a tied vote, whereupon the President awarded his casting vote to the opposition, which usually indicated that in his view they had spoken more persuasively. In a reporter's opinion Storey's contribution 'was informative and refreshing'. Early in the New Year following this debut he was asked to join the Board of Six which organised College debates.

In February 1935 he spoke in favour of a motion supporting the League of Nations, which was carried comfortably. During the rest of his time at Stonyhurst he appeared on the order paper three times. Even at this stage of his life he was not afraid to take an independent line. In October 1935 the reporter of a debate on a motion critical of Italy's policy in Abyssinia, which was narrowly defeated, scornfully described Storey's views as 'unmistakably Communistic'. 'Italy had no land, Abyssinia had

*9: Stonyhurst: an Officer Training Corps Camp, n.d.
(Storey at the back).*

plenty of wasted land. Why should not Italy take over some of Abyssinia's apparently unwanted territory?' There is no hint as to why he came to this viewpoint, which, though scarcely Communistic, was certainly naïve. To judge from the number of votes cast, debating was not the most popular activity at Stonyhurst. For Storey, however, it was something at which he eventually became adept, and which he always enjoyed.

Other extra-curricular activities included playing a number of small parts in a production of 'Macbeth' in 1935; and also in that year, appearing in the pantomime 'Aladdin' performed by the Officer Training Corps. He showed no particular aptitude for stage work or liking for the Corps, leaving the latter after the compulsory year with a routine Certificate of Efficiency. Ever since his experiences with Bullen, the Drill Master at Bishop's

Court, he had been sceptical about militarism in any guise. According to one contemporary, John Page, who later had a distinguished career in the army, Stonyhurst 'in the 1930s was… .an overtly militaristic school (with an OTC which was second-to-none in the national competitions)'. Storey recognised that this was part of the College's wholehearted acceptance of public school norms, but would have regarded as incongruous the OTC's involvement in religious ceremonies at Easter and on the feast of Corpus Christi.

On the other hand, he was thoroughly enthused by another opportunity which was entirely voluntary. Particularly during the 1930s, there was a strong resurgence of Catholicism in England, with around 12,000 converts each year. Having a long tradition of engaging in proselytisation, the Jesuits were closely involved and Fr. Martin D'Arcy, the Bishop's Court and Stonyhurst Old Boy, was prominent. Storey was aware of this and during 1934-35, and again in 1935-36, he sat the Inter-Collegiate Examination in Religious Knowledge (otherwise known as the Higher Religious Certificate) and reached the credit, or approved, standard on each occasion. The examination was in Christian Apologetics. There was also a practical test in which candidates had to articulate, and to defend under interrogation, a particular aspect of the Catholic faith, Storey's choice being 'Infallibility', for which he no doubt drew on his debating experience.

The Certificate had been established under the auspices of the Conference of Catholic Colleges, of which Stonyhurst was a member. Its objective was to equip students 'to meet the doubts and questionings of an unbelieving age' and during its inaugural year in 1921 the first prize had been awarded to a Stonyhurst pupil. It was hoped that those who passed the Certificate would become members of the Catholic Evidence Guild, of which there was a branch at Stonyhust. We do not know precisely why Storey took the course twice in consecutive years, but the knowledge and skill he acquired were regularly employed in later years. He lost no time in becoming a member of the Guild. He probably regarded the Higher Religious Certificate (and had been encouraged by the College to do so) as preparing him for Catholic Action, then being encouraged by Pope Pius XI. Beginning in Italy as the Church's response to the growth of Fascism, it soon spread elsewhere. Catholic Action was certainly something which Storey strongly supported and sought to popularise as a curate in Middlesbrough after the war.

While not accepting uncritically everything with which he was confronted - few pupils did - he gained a great deal from the Jesuits. The only downside of his time at Stonyhurst was a further brief experience of bullying, again on his own part against a friend. He was always deeply ashamed of this and afterwards steered clear of it by loosely associating himself with one of the 'gangs' among the boys. He always spoke fondly of his time at Stonyhurst. The Society of Jesus had a deserved reputation for its concern for the liberty of the individual, as did Storey through his early membership of Amnesty International and his later work for justice and peace in the diocese of Middlesbrough. Among the leading organisations in Jesuit schools was the Sodality of Our Lady, an adaptation of the lay brotherhoods and confraternities so popular in Catholic Europe during and since the middle ages. The Sodality was important and influential in the religious life of the school. While Storey's Marian devotion originated with his mother, it was firmly consolidated at Stonyhurst: the rosary was among his favourite forms of prayer and following his ordination he was a frequent visitor to Lourdes. Another devotion, and a characteristically Jesuit one, was that to Christ the King, whose 'call' featured at the heart of the *Spiritual Exercises* of St. Ignatius Loyola, founder of the Jesuits. The feast of Christ the King had been established by Pope Pius XI in 1925. The strong Jesuit commitment to this particular devotion left its mark on Storey. Years later, in private correspondence with a very close friend, both regularly referred to 'His Majesty' and 'Her Majesty' in discussing Christ and his mother, Mary. Moreover, the entire approach to education of the Jesuits strongly supported his personal determination to get to the bottom of things in regard to his faith. Above all, while at Stonyhurst he never lost the sense that he might have a vocation to the priesthood. Many priests had been, and continued to be, educated and later ordained at the College, as he was. Though it had seen even better days before the Great War, Stonyhurst in his time was a lively and successful institution which stretched its pupils intellectually and physically; and which undoubtedly strengthened and developed their spiritual lives.

After a year in 'Upper Poetry', Storey left Stonyhurst on 27 July 1936. He was then not quite seventeen-and-a-half years old and on the verge of manhood. Later, looking back on his childhood and schooldays, what struck him most forcibly was the preponderance of males in his life. This was generally true, but especially so of his own family, with an older sister, Agatha, who was obliged 'to join in the farming exercise', and a younger one, Patience, who was still a child when he left for Rome. His education had been all-male and girls had played virtually no part in the rest of his life – 'I never knew a girl of any kind'. He had attended the occasional, very formal dance with little or no enjoyment. The only instruction he received about sex came from his brother, John, home on a brief visit.

It was about what happened and what it was about: nothing to do with love, of course, it was simply about the machinery and how sex worked….my instruction about relationships or learning how to love was absolutely meaningless – it didn't exist.

48

It was precisely because Aelred of Rievaulx and Erich Fromm later filled this gap that he so revered their writings.

Inevitably, there were occasions when hormones kicked in which, far from forgetting, he recalled in some detail. Aged about fifteen or sixteen, he had attended a point-to-point meeting near Warter and was standing near the sixth fence when Malise, a niece of Lady Nun, rode past on a lovely chestnut horse.

> [She] rounded the corner....with such grace and beauty, and zoomed past and I was electrified and I suppose this is what we call Eros - Cupid with his bow. I had never spoken to her in my life and I never spoke to her afterwards. All I know is I was absolutely shattered. All the way home....my father was saying 'you're very silent' and I had nothing to say. I just didn't know what it meant. I was just absolutely taken.

Incidents like this occasionally invaded his 'very much male world'.

As the 1930s proceeded that world became increasingly uncertain and insecure. Storey sensed this without getting regular or precise information about what was going on. However, while the rise of Fascism somewhat passed him by at this stage, he picked up gossip about the relationship between Wallis Simpson and the King which led eventually to the latter's abdication. Above all, the economic difficulties facing farming became obvious as his older brothers, all of whom except Peter wanted to pursue careers in agriculture, strove to make their way in the world. Gerard had taken a degree in agriculture at Leeds University but after graduation failed to find an opening. Eventually he took a short-service commission in the R.A.F. and when the war started was stationed in Iraq, then a British Protectorate, training Iraqi pilots. Nor could the next brother, John, get into agriculture. He joined the police in Palestine and until the war worked as a senior security officer at Tel Aviv airport, regularly being covered at Christmas by his Jewish colleagues while he went to Bethlehem for the Nativity Mass. After studying at the London School of Economics Agatha became an almoner in a London hospital; and Peter, always set on the priesthood, was an early entrant from Stonyhurst to Ushaw College. Aidan went off to military duties in India and lost a leg there in a bizarre shooting incident before the war when, as an officer, he attempted to save some of his men after an Indian soldier had begun randomly shooting his colleagues. This was a singularly depressing catalogue, not least for George Storey, who at some point in the 1930s seriously considered emigrating with his family to Australia. In the event, after Lady Nun's death he stayed on at Warter Priory under the new owners. Then in 1938, in his early sixties, he moved back to work on the much smaller property of his former employer, Lady Herries, at Everingham Park.

This was the troubled background to Storey's own decision to test the possibility of his having a vocation to the priesthood. We do not know when he finally determined to do so, though his decision seems to have flowed from the incident with the Mill Hill Father at Bishop's Court, and then to have lain dormant for several years. His choice of subjects for his Higher School Certificate, which included Latin and Greek, is not revealing because in his day the majority of students at Stonyhurst, and certainly the ablest, proceeded on the classical side. On the other hand taking the Higher School Certificate in Religious Knowledge twice in consecutive years suggests a growing seriousness about his faith. It is a pity that we know so little about the background to his father's advice that he become a solicitor or join the navy. Perhaps George feared a repeat of his own experience in going to Ushaw or that Storey was merely copying his older brother, Peter, about whose likely future there seems to have been no doubt. His parents had never considered Storey as a candidate for the priesthood and his decision to become one

10: Family Photograph before Storey's departure for Rome,
1936. (Back row: Aidan, Agatha, Storey, Peter.
Middle Row: Gerard, George, Harriet, John.
Front Row: Cinders, Patience).

came like a bolt from the blue, though we do not know when they
learned of it. It was his brother, Peter, who supported Storey's
decision to proceed to the seminary.

In photographs of Storey at Stonyhurst and in Rome, he
often appears unsmiling and sometimes grave, as if he had a lot
on his mind. And indeed proceeding to the English College was
a very serious step which would not have been contemplated
without very careful thought by Storey himself, by his parents
and by the ecclesiastical authorities. The admissions record of
the English College casts no light on the matter, merely noting
that in October 1936 Storey 'entered the Ven. College from the
parish of Pocklington in the diocese of Middlesbrough, for the

same diocese'. According to Storey, the decision to proceed there 'came to me quite suddenly'. While it is clear that both his parents thought it an unwise move, once he had made up his mind they too supported him. It is also clear, however, that throughout his seminary training the final outcome of his decision remained in doubt as far as he himself was concerned.

Inevitably, during his last days at Stonyhurst, there was much talk among his fellow leavers as to what they intended to do. One of his friends was incredulous about Storey's own plan, which seems to confirm that it was a sudden decision about which he was discreet.

'Storey, you can't possibly be going off to be a priest. How ridiculous! Do you mean that you're never going to live with a girl?' It seemed to me an extraordinary question. 'Live with girls?' Girls didn't come into my life at all that far.

None of them realised that within a few years the world would be plunged into war, but as this possibility became reality, questions arose about their choices and many plans were changed. Among those whose details we have and who were admitted to Stonyhurst along with Storey in 1932, at least 16 subsequently served in the armed forces. Three of them - John Page, Charles Bewlay and Brian Devlin - stayed on after the war and made a career in the army. Three others were killed on active service. The other Old Boys survived after serving in various capacities and locations. One staff member well-known to Storey, Fr. Walkerley, also survived after serving as a Chaplain with the R.A.F. As we will see, there were others of Storey's acquaintance who joined the forces, and some of whom were killed in hostilities. In the years after Stonyhurst he came to ponder his own choice repeatedly while still failing to persuade himself completely that he should become a priest.

CHAPTER THREE
SEMINARY

In the late summer of 1936 the young man who travelled to the English College in Rome to embark on a seven-year course of training for the priesthood – citing a desire to see the Christian faith recovered - immediately encountered experiences quite beyond his ken. He had never previously been abroad and the journey by train, boat and train was by far his longest to date. Three years later another aspirant, Michael Killeen, spent five days on the journey from Leeds to Rome, staying overnight in London and Paris. Storey's experience was probably similar. Having always lived rurally, Rome was a revelation to him, although years later he had virtually nothing to say about it.

> Going to Rome was a great experience: no point in trying to describe the effect of Rome and St. Peter's and the whole city on a young man of 17 as I was…It's been done by so many people.

This may have been modesty; or, more likely, an inability adequately to capture the impact on a budding seminarian who had led a sheltered life of a first encounter with the eternal city. His sole recorded memory is of black prisoners-of-war - from Italy's conflict in Abyssinia - at the city's railway station. He had never previously seen a black person, 'except in Bertram Mills' circus'.

The English College remains the oldest English institution in Continental Europe. Founded in 1362 as a hospice for English pilgrims to Rome, it became a seminary during the Elizabethan persecution of the later 16th century. Since then it had shared the city's many vicissitudes and under Napoleon had only narrowly escaped confiscation and abolition. Student numbers had fluctuated, though they were often modest before the 20th century and fell to 15 during the Great War. Thereafter they recovered rapidly and were 60-80 throughout the inter-war period.

Having known Warter Priory as a child and lived at Stonyhurst for four years, Storey was perhaps less impressed by the College's buildings than many of his colleagues, but there was much for him to admire nonetheless. Situated in the Via di Monserrato in the medieval heart of Rome near the River Tiber, its fine church had been largely rebuilt during the later 19th century. More recently, under the rectorship of Arthur Hinsley (1917-29), other areas, including the main corridor on the ground floor, the Library, and the Common Room, had been substantially reconstructed or remodelled. In addition the church had been provided with a new organ, central heating had been installed, and a swimming tank had been erected in the garden.

While these changes were underway Italian politics underwent a revolution from the right which brought Mussolini and his Fascists to power. Many Catholics, including British ones, were broadly supportive of this development as a bulwark against the threat of Bolshevism. In Italy under Mussolini government action was frequently arbitrary, always unpredictable, and often involved the suspension of democratic processes; but there were also achievements. Schemes for water regulation, land reclamation and mountain conservation bore considerable fruit. Together with new insecticides from Britain and America, they combined steadily to eradicate the ancient scourge of malaria. Progress in communications was considerable. Some 5,000 kilometres of rail track were electrified by 1939 and many of the main cities and tourist centres were linked by *autostrade*. And the government generated 'a veritable building fever' in the major urban areas. Much less impressive was the regime's haphazard and aggressive foreign policy, which led to a sharp decline in Italian influence overseas and which, in the case of Mussolini's colonial endeavours in Africa, created outright opposition from the League of Nations, including sanctions from Britain.

In 1929, after decades of stand-off between the two, there was a major reconciliation between the Catholic Church and the Italian State via the Lateran Treaty and an accompanying Concordat. Pope Pius XI formally recognised the existence of the Italian State and the Italian occupation of Rome. The Church retained only the sovereign territory of the Vatican, and Catholicism was confirmed as the official religion with a call on government protection. While there were other concessions – legal, financial and educational – the Church paid an increasingly heavy price for its new status. As a corollary of establishment the State kept a tight grip on the Church, including a voice in ecclesiastical nominations. Mussolini repeatedly pursued policies inimical to the spirit, if not the letter, of the agreement, for example by fiercely attacking Catholic Action: subsequently the work of Catholic organisations in the training of young people seriously diminished. From time to time the Church voiced reservations about the government's more strident views and activities, but in general supported the authoritarian regime. The growth of Mussolini's power derived not inconsiderably from Catholic support.

There is no means of determining how conversant Storey was with all this by 1936. In England upper middle-class Catholic opinion was firmly on the right politically and his position is unlikely to have been different. On arrival in Rome his knowledge and understanding of what was happening both in Italy and elsewhere in Europe seems to have been rudimentary. From this point onwards, however, a growing interest in current affairs, particularly insofar as they impinged on his religious beliefs, was never in doubt. A dominant personal recollection of the next few years was of his education, from a very low base, in what was happening in Europe and internationally.

The various national Colleges, of which the English College was merely one, provided the city with a cosmopolitan group of seminarians. Among Storey's colleagues, views and political affiliations were diverse, and some were extraordinarily ignorant. Hugh Lavery, an exact contemporary in Rome and later a lifelong friend, was dismayed by the 'John Bull parochialism' evident among some members of English College, who regarded Italy's imperial ambitions as outrageous: and they themselves felt it 'unpatriotic to show interest in any other country, in its history, its art, [and] its achievements'. In the wider student body there were fiercely conflicting ideologies and a series of major international developments provoked intense discussion, sometimes further stimulated by events in Rome itself. Together with some of his colleagues, Storey took to listening to Mussolini holding forth in Rome's central hub, the Piazza Venezia; and there is little doubt that it was primarily his experience of Italian Fascism which fostered a firm and permanent belief that State and Church should be clearly separated. He remained sympathetic, however, to Mussolini's complaint that, while Britain controlled much of Africa, Italy faced sanctions and the wrath of the League of Nations because of its activities in Abyssinia. As at Stonyhurst, such a view would not have endeared him to many, if any, of his colleagues.

Soon there came news of the starvation of millions in the Ukraine as a result of Stalin's enforcement of farm collectivisation. In view of Communism's long-term objective of taking over the world, many contemporaries wondered whether Nazism and Fascism were indeed unwholesome, or whether they were necessary buffers against a larger threat from the east; a threat which, with its associated atheism, was keenly felt among seminarians. The arguments which swirled around this issue were brought into sharp focus by the civil war in Spain (1936-39) which, according to Storey, 'divided us'. Whether in saying that he was referring to the English College alone, to the wider body of seminarians in Rome, or to both is uncertain. There is no doubt that the dominant feeling in the English College was pro-Nationalist; and the fall of Barcelona and then of Madrid to Franco's forces were celebrated with mealtime distributions of extra wine. But there were sharp differences of opinion on many issues, both within and between the Colleges. Moreover, as tensions mounted throughout Europe, the views of individuals changed. Michael Killeen, three years behind Storey, regarded him at that early stage as 'a staunch supporter of justice', possibly as a result of joint involvement in group discussions about the social teaching of the Church via the earlier encyclicals *Rerum Novarum* and *Quadragesimo Anno*.

Storey's routine at the College was very similar to that of many previous generations of students. Seminaries had long been and for many years remained closed institutions. Only following the deliberations of the Second Vatican Council was there significant reform of their system. Each student had his own room, and each was allocated a priest confessor who was also his spiritual director. Daily life was disciplined and uniform with a regular pattern of prayer, study and recreation. Students were roused by a bell at 5.30 am and had half an hour's meditation before Mass and a sparse breakfast. They then walked to the Gregorian University where they attended four forty-five minute lectures. They returned to the College where they prayed for the conversion of England, had lunch and then relaxed in the Common Room. During the afternoon they got some exercise, walking in the city to some place of interest or

11: English College: Storey in his First Year, 1936-37.

engaging in sporting activity. The service of Benediction preceded supper after which everyone, including the Rector and his colleagues, gathered in the Common Room, where smoking was permitted. Following the communal singing of the *Salve Regina,* they retired to their rooms at 9.00 pm.

Special rules applied outside the College, with normal dress being a black soutane and a broad-brimmed hat (*saturno*). Students were not allowed to leave the College on their own or with a single other colleague, but always *in camerata,* i.e. in groups of three or more. Grumbles about restrictions, and over the decades there were many, were countered by statements that adherence to the rules was character-forming. Successive Rectors and Vice-Rectors engendered the spirit of their respective regimes – some were strict and others more relaxed – but similarities significantly outweighed differences. When Storey arrived, William Godfrey (later Cardinal Archbishop of Westminster 1956-63) was Rector. Under him discipline was strictly enforced, not least because there was pressure from the Vatican Congregation for Seminaries and Studies for it to be so, and Godfrey was ambitious.

College life, therefore, was largely cut off from the outside world and there was little, if any, contact with Italian Catholics. Complementing the jingoistic attitudes deplored by Hugh Lavery, hardly anyone learned Italian. Storey did so, however: no doubt slowly due to the limited opportunities in seminary life, but eventually to the point where he became reasonably comfortable with, though by no means fluent, in the language. The daily routine was steeped in tradition and elements within it were slow to change. Parts of meals were taken in silence while public reading took place. In Storey's time a common text, with 'hobnailed prose' in a 'leaden translation', was *The Lives of the Popes* by the Austrian historian, Ludwig von Pastor. To

12: English College: Skiing on the slopes of Mt. Terminillo, Christmas/New Year, 1936-37 (Storey on far left).

everyone's relief the Rector who succeeded Godfrey in 1940, Monsignor John MacMillan, dropped it in favour of Apsley Cherry-Garrard's Antarctic epic, *The Worst Journey in the World.* Once a month, guided excursions to places of local interest were arranged; and there were opportunities during vacations, particularly after Easter and in late August, to explore Italy beyond Rome. Storey had an early break. Together with some of his colleagues, he went skiing on the slopes of Mount Terminillo in the Appenines, some 60 miles from Rome, over Christmas and New Year 1936-37. During the stifling heat of August the entire College migrated to the Villa Palazzola. Bought cheaply in 1920 by the Rector, Arthur Hinsley, this property lay in a beautiful location above Lake Albano in the Alban Hills, 18 miles from the city centre and just across a valley from the papal summer residence at Castelgandolfo.

Storey settled into life at the College without undue difficulty. As he had spent the previous eight years living communally, this was easier for him than others. He was used to rubbing shoulders with people whose views and temperaments were different from his own. He also learned a good deal from his brother Peter who had arrived from Ushaw in 1934 and continued until his own ordination in 1941. Storey acted as Infirmarian, probably to his year group, for his first three years and then, perhaps because of his experience at Stonyhurst, was appointed Secretary to the College's Debating Society for 1940-41. It is unfortunate that no records of the Society's activities are available for this period to set alongside those for Stonyhurst and for Christ's College: but it is safe to assume that there was no gap in his participation in debating.

Some of the texture of his life at the College can be gleaned from references to him and his brother in *Chi Lo Sa,* the satirical magazine published by the students three times a year, although some material consisted of in-jokes difficult for outsiders to comprehend. Peter seems to have gained a reputation as a fresh-air fanatic, the virtues of which were not always appreciated in the depths of an Italian winter. Another reference, to the bluntness of his razor-blades, is explained by a cartoon showing Peter with a beard and with both brothers in pyjamas, underneath the caption 'Two Bedtime Storeys''. Almost inevitably, Storey regularly faced ribaldry because of his remarkably aquiline nose. Nor is it surprising that there were comments on his love of rugby and his strength as a player. On one occasion the Editor felt obliged to point out to him that Benedict XV was not a rugby team; and on another, above the caption 'Lie on Storey again boys!', a cartoon shows him prone beneath several members of an opposing side. This last item has all the players wearing the sort of kit normally associated with a fully competitive match, so his rugby playing in Rome may have been on more than a purely recreational basis.

During their seven years in residence students were allowed to return home for a single summer vacation. This was usually at the end of their third year, between their study of philosophy and of theology, though for some reason Storey had his break in 1938, after his second year in Rome. Years later, not long before his death, he maintained that on two occasions he had nearly been expelled from the College for expressing views that were critical of aspects of Church policy. Perhaps this early break was designed as an opportunity for him to reflect on his position.

While in England he went to visit an aunt in Lancashire and she took him to Blackpool to see Sonja Henie, the Norwegian figure skater and film star, who was on an exhibition tour of Britain. Once again, he was transfixed by the sight of a beautiful woman.

> Suddenly seeing this girl I was absolutely completely taken and I remember my aunt saying 'Anthony, you do realise you can't look at girls like that'. I didn't realise I was looking at her like anything. All I knew was I was absolutely glued to this incredible figure, and that too stayed in my mind for a long time.

Episodes like this might have had sufficient impact to be noticed by those accompanying him, but did not encourage him to alter his chosen course.

There was serious academic work to be done – the three years of philosophy and four years of theology required of all students for the priesthood. Like everyone else at the English College, Storey studied at the Gregorian, the Pontifical University founded and still largely staffed by the Jesuits. All lectures were in Latin, and all communication between teachers and students was in that language. Although this was one of the six subjects in which Storey had passed his Higher School Certificate, this requirement was daunting, not least because most professors spoke too rapidly to be readily understood. The only consolation for Storey was that most of his colleagues had a similar, if not more difficult, mountain to climb. Another problem was equally fundamental. There were some thousands of clerical students in Rome. Individual lectures were often attended by upwards of 200 of them and there was little, if any, interaction between teachers and students, although all examinations were oral. The Italian mode of learning was very much by rote and intellectual attitudes were extremely conservative. Lectures were in effect dictations and named textbooks were regarded as of paramount importance: any other reading was strictly supplementary, secondary and in no way a replacement. Moreover, when they got back to the College students were expected to copy up their lecture notes. According to Michael Killeen, 'those students were best thought of who learnt best by heart'. There was 'little relationship between the learning imparted at the University and the students' day-to-day interests….the whole purpose of the course was to initiate into the received viewpoint'. Killeen was a very bright young man and had been a high-flying student at St. Michael's Jesuit College in Leeds, fluent in Latin on arrival in Rome. Yet, despite his command of that language, he struggled with the content of the Philosophy lectures at the Gregorian and felt an overwhelming sense of relief on being obliged, as we will see, to continue his studies in England after only a year.

With additional experience of the system at the Gregorian, Storey cast the net of his criticism rather more widely. He often found himself bored and frustrated and his courses uninteresting.

I don't think I met any scholarship in Rome at all and no openness to things. All our history of everything was always

*13: English College: Group Photograph, 1938
(Storey far left of 7, 2nd row from back).
The four Superiors in the middle of the front row are (from
left) Monsignor Elwes, Monsignor Godfrey, Rector, Cardinal
Hinsley, and Monsignor Smith, Vice-Rector.*

from the view of the Catholic Church. We were quite narrow-minded really, and always talking about other people as though they were wicked and sinful.

A few years after Storey's time, in the 1950s, Cormac Murphy-O'Connor, the future Cardinal Archbishop of Westminster, was also critical.

I can't say that I much enjoyed my studies at the Gregorian ….We sat on desks and we took notes. Or we fell asleep … . sometimes - if I had any money - I would just slope off and have a coffee or a bun or something. I was usually hungry.

It was perhaps unsurprising that clerical academics in Italy, locked within a rigid system, were like this because, in terms of religious belief, Catholics were in a majority in that country. Having been a member of a small minority in England and encountered no prejudice because of this, Storey knew that some of the assumptions which underlay Italian attitudes and approaches were questionable. Nevertheless, he was much more accepting of conventional orthodoxy than he was later to become and seems to have experienced little difficulty in satisfying his examiners. Two years after arriving in Rome, he successfully completed his Baccalaureate in Philosophy; and a year later he was awarded a Licentiate in the subject.

In 1938 Storey had arrived back in England for a summer break just as the Prime Minister, Neville Chamberlain, returned from meeting Hitler at Berchtesgaden, bringing with him the promise of 'peace in our time'. During the next academic year, following his return to the English College, 'things began to hot up'. In January 1939 Hitler visited Mussolini in Rome. Anxious to get a glimpse of them if possible, Storey and a colleague encountered both – 'funny little men they were' - as the two leaders, having had an audience with King Victor Emmanuel, came down the steps of the Quirinal Palace. He maintained that it might have been useful for him to have had a bomb to hand on that occasion. 'I'm not sure whether it would have helped me very much but it might have changed things'. A month later Chamberlain came out to Rome with Lord Halifax. The students were introduced to them, but unsurprisingly Halifax failed to recognise the young huntsman who had opened gates for him back in the East Riding. It was at this time, February 1939, that Storey joined some of his colleagues in forming one of the guard of honour round the coffin of Pope Pius XI at the lying-in-state which preceded his funeral.

Storey had begun his theological studies at the English College in the late summer of 1939, just before the outbreak of

14: English College: Lord Halifax's Visit, February 1939.

war between Britain and Germany, but did not complete them there. Although in consultation with the Vatican and the English hierarchy Monsignor MacMillan took various precautions, his policy was to continue as normal if at all possible, unless Italy declared war on Britain. Mussolini had formally allied with Hitler through the Pact of Steel in May 1939, but hesitated to go further, being jealous of Hitler's success and conscious that his country was ill-prepared to enter full-blown hostilities. Treatment of Britain in the Italian press remained moderate in tone and Italian public opinion was decidedly anti-war. Only more than a year later, on 10 June 1940, did Italy formally declare war on Britain and France. In early May 1940, as tensions rose inexorably towards the end of this long period of prevarication, Storey got involved in a very dangerous situation – so dangerous that he might have been badly beaten, taken into custody or worse.

On 9 April 15,000 German troops invaded Norway and Denmark, catching Britain completely by surprise. Only four days earlier British ships had set out to lay mines in Norwegian waters and Neville Chamberlain had declared that 'Hitler has missed the bus'. It was at this point that anti-British propaganda in Italy intensified. Posters appeared in the streets of Rome throwing the same words back at Britain: '*Inghilterra ha perduto l'autobus*', to which many students at the College took great exception. There are slightly conflicting reports as to precisely what happened next, though there is no doubt that Storey was centrally involved. One version claimed that he tore down a poster which had appeared on a College wall. Another maintained that he and three other students removed a number of posters from various locations in the city. Retailing the story in later years, his memory was that he did so in company with a single student friend, Timothy Walker. Shortly afterwards the police arrived at the College. They knew about the incident and that College students had been responsible. In the absence of the Rector, the Vice-Rector, Monsignor Richard Smith, recognised that the situation was exceedingly dangerous as German police were already in the city. We do not know exactly what he did, but Joseph Holland, a seminarian from Southport who was in Storey's year-group, subsequently reported that 'with difficulty [Monsignor Smith] saved some lads who had torn down..[posters]..from the clutches of the Fascists'. About a week later, as the situation continued to deteriorate, most of the staff and all the students at the English College were evacuated from Italy.

After Germany invaded Holland, Belgium and Luxembourg on 10 May, Monsignor Smith set in motion preparations for likely evacuation. These intensified over the next few days and he announced his decision to evacuate on the evening of 14 May. The following day saw a maelstrom of last-minute activity and at 8.25 am on the 16th, in a carriage reserved for them by Thomas Cook's agent in the city, members of the College departed on what turned out to be the very last train from Rome to Paris. They encountered no difficulty when they crossed the Italian border; later they passed through Dijon as the German army was breaking through the Maginot Line at Sedan. Having seen newspapers reporting their retreat, along with those of Scottish and Canadian seminarians, they arrived in Paris on the following afternoon and booked into a hotel near the Gare du Nord. They spent the next twenty-four hours killing time in the centre of Paris, with some (including Storey) watching Zoltan Korda's film 'The Four Feathers' in a cinema on the Champs Elysees during an air-raid. Later, in another reserved carriage and with major detours and many delays, they travelled that night to Le Havre where, at 2 am the following morning, 19 May, they caught the last civil boat, a ferry, to leave the port before the harbour was mined. In his exhausted state Storey failed to register whether they docked at Southampton or Portsmouth, but Joe Holland reported them sailing 'up Southampton Water [on a] lovely sunny Sunday'. On the train to London the two of them discussed the possible make-up from among their group of a cricket team for the summer. They arrived in London in the early evening, with the northern contingent staying overnight in the Russell Hotel in Russell Square. On the following morning those who had yet to travel on gathered for Mass in Westminster Cathedral and then went home.

Throughout this period and beyond the dilemma for many seminarians as the crisis deepened was whether, if circumstances permitted, they should continue with their studies, which were classified as a 'reserved occupation'; or whether they should relinquish them and join the war effort. Timothy Walker was a case in point. His mother was a Catholic, he had been sent to Eton, and was already reading the bible in Hebrew when he first arrived at the English College. There, according to *Chi Lo Sa,* he was known as 'Waterloo' because the battle, according to some, had been won on Eton's playing fields. Storey was one of Timothy's many friends: in his view, aside from other qualities, Timothy was 'a great nature man....able to handle snakes in the mountains'. Walker's father was a Captain in the Royal Navy who went on to win numerous decorations for sinking U-boats and about whom several books were subsequently published. During the early months of the war he urged his son to join the navy, whereupon Timothy solicited advice from his ultimate ecclesiastical superior, Cardinal Hinsley. The sympathetic reply left the matter entirely in Timothy's hands. He left the College, joined the navy as a submariner and, having embarked on his first voyage in the *Thetis* (which had been sunk, raised, and refurbished), he and the rest of the crew were never seen again. It is clear from the way in which Storey discussed the issues surrounding this episode that, despite his ambivalence towards armed conflict, he himself was in turmoil over it and thought long and hard about joining the armed forces. While he did not do so, a good number of others did and some of them lost their lives in the conflict. There is no doubt that this was one of the factors which underlay his hesitancy to proceed to ordination; and it continued to trouble him.

After reaching London in May 1940 the students of the repatriated English College were not only exhausted; they also:

> felt terribly down. Everyone was urging everyone else to stick together & keep [the] Coll[ege] going somehow & collecting addresses to keep in touch.

They need not have worried. Monsignor Macmillan had been in England for some months and got back to Rome only on the eve of the repatriation. He and his superiors in the hierarchy had concluded some time earlier, though they kept it to themselves,

15: Croft Lodge, Ambleside 1940.

that the College would eventually have to be evacuated from Rome. This was why he was absent when the posters were torn down and why the crisis had to be dealt with by his Vice-Rector.

Following excellent preparatory work by the Vice-Rector, Macmillan had been on a scouting mission to identify accommodation suitable for a repatriated College. After a short break at home staff and students were housed in the Lake District at Croft Lodge, Ambleside, in Monsignor Smith's home diocese of Lancaster. This was a Victorian country house overlooking Windermere, sub-let by the tenant (who retained the first floor) to the Catholic Holiday Guild, from whom the College leased it for six weeks. According to Hugh Lavery, 'though a large house', the Lodge 'was a small College', and arrangements were decidedly makeshift. Together with the administrator of Lancaster Cathedral, the local parish priest, Fr. Atkinson, helped in various ways. The students themselves plugged the many gaps arising from the wartime shortage of domestic help. A skeleton teaching staff, augmented by a few volunteers from the diocese, delivered a truncated programme of study. It even proved possible to publish a number of *Chi Lo Sa.* In keeping the College together following a traumatic move amidst an international crisis, this stop-gap fulfilled its purpose. And as every afternoon was free, there were plenty of opportunities for students to get out and about, rowing on the lake, fishing, and climbing Great Gable, Helvellyn, Scafell Pike or the Langdales. Subsequently Storey held the Lake District very dear and visited it repeatedly for the rest of his life.

For several months Britain faced an ever-increasing threat of German invasion. When Storey got back to the East Riding he joined the Everingham unit of the newly-established Local Defence Volunteers, soon called the Home Guard, and later 'Dads' Army'. He served with the unit both before and after his stay at Croft Lodge. By this time his father had left Warter Priory and returned to his previous post as agent for Lady Herries at Everingham Park where, as at Warter, he also farmed. There by mid-1940, in addition to his other responsibilities, George Storey was Area Warden for the village. Storey's youthful experience on a great shooting estate was immediately put to good use. Along with Storr, the groom at Everingham, he cleaned guns, newly arrived from Canada, and prepared cartridges for them; and also cartridges, suitably adapted for use against paratroops, for local shotguns. Less useful, indeed 'very sad', was the task of helping Scottish soldiers fell great oak trees in Dog Kennel Wood at Everingham. Minesweepers were in short supply and, to evade damage from the mines they were seeking, minesweepers were best built of wood. In addition, on one occasion his unit practised with a bomb designed to be stuck onto the side of an invading tank. A tree stood in for the tank but, on being attached and activated, the bomb failed to detonate and a disposal unit had to be called out from Beverley.

Meanwhile, rationing was in full swing and all manner of things became scarce. His mother sometimes sent him out to shoot a rabbit for dinner; and once, seeing a stag at the edge of a wood in Everingham, he shot that too, though not very cleanly. He vowed never to kill a deer again and, salving his conscience somewhat, shared out the venison amongst the villagers. Not that far away, Hull was being heavily bombed and George and Harriet Storey took in two young female evacuees. There were occasional flurries of activity as Spitfires roared across the sky to tackle a German attack on Driffield airbase; or as German aircraft, having dropped their lethal loads on Hull, turned for home over the East Riding, with searchlights playing around them from Market Weighton, Holme-on-Spalding-Moor and Everingham itself. Most dramatic of all was a false alarm in the middle of the night that the east coast was being invaded. Storey mustered with a 2.2 rifle, one colleague had a Ross rifle but only ten rounds of ammunition, another had a pistol, and the other two had a scythe and a sickle respectively.

> There was no hatred for the Germans at all; they were just going to get killed....each village was going to have to kill as many Germans as they could as they moved on through. It was a lovely morning I remember..... The only enemy we saw was a hedgehog, which we duly didn't kill, and it crossed the road in front of us.

Storey's verdict on this tense period was succinct. 'Dads [Army] wasn't a joke at all, but it was very funny'. However, his military duties could be undertaken only at periods of great crisis or during vacations, for the bulk of his theological studies had yet to be completed.

16: Stonyhurst: St. Mary's Hall. 1940-43.

What happened next was in many ways even more impressive than the exodus from Rome. Seeking as close a link as possible with the Jesuits, Monsignor MacMillan had approached them for help. Just before the students left Croft Lodge for a longer break at home he announced that the Provincial of the English Jesuits had agreed to allow the College to take over St. Mary's Hall at Stonyhurst, a substantial building, separate from the school, which until the move to Heythrop had been the Jesuit novitiate. It had then lain empty for several years before being requisitioned by the military who, after representations by the Vice-Rector, were about to leave. In addition, though the Jesuits were badly stretched for personnel, they provided a fine group of professors to staff St. Mary's, including some who had previously taught in Rome. And following detailed negotiations and under strict controls, the Gregorian delegated to the relocated College responsibility for the teaching and examination of its students.

It was fortunate that classes in Rome had continued till May, so little if anything had been lost from the previous year's work. An advance party of students spent some weeks preparing St. Mary's for its new occupants and the rest of the College arrived in late September. A routine as close as possible to that previously followed in Rome was re-established and lasted until 1946. There were significant differences however. Stonyhurst was in the depths of the north Lancashire countryside, without ready access to the workers and facilities available in a major city. Among the offices which the students discharged in filling the gaps – and some were dismayed at being obliged to do so - were those of gardener, coalman, house cleaner, furniture man, refectory man and, in wartime of course, black-out man. Thus, Storey returned to familiar surroundings at Stonyhurst, very close to his Lancashire relatives, and not too far from his family home in the East Riding, where his father's health was beginning to falter after years of struggling with agriculture's problems.

Storey paid eloquent testimony to the significance for him of the next three years.

> Our studies were taken very seriously. I did enjoy them… .and….learnt far more theology and everything else during that time than I did while I was in Rome. I really became interested both in theological questions and faith questions; and also sociology and the nature of Fascism and Marxism.

The clear implication of these remarks is that previously he had not found himself seriously engaged with or interested in such matters, particularly the latter. He had some gifted and inspiring teachers, including Fr. Bernard Leeming who had taught at the Gregorian during the mid-1930s and was to earn a formidable reputation as a scholar and writer in the post-war period. He paid particularly warm tribute to two others, both of whom, he felt, were a distinct cut above anyone else he had previously encountered: they too had been repatriated from Rome but their strongest influence on him was at St. Mary's Hall. One was a German Jew who became a Catholic priest and held a Doctorate in Theology from the University of Innsbruck: Fr. Engelbert Gutwenger, who, though he taught Storey only briefly, was in his view 'a very good theologian'. He reserved his highest praise, however, for Fr. Robert Dyson, who was born in England but whose family had moved to the United States when he was a child. He attended Boston College, Massachusetts, became a Jesuit and taught Classics there before taking up Theology in Naples and then Biblical Studies in Rome. After holding a Chair in Scripture back in the States during the mid-1930s, he was appointed Professor in the Pontifical Biblical Institute at the Gregorian. At St. Mary's Hall Fr. Dyson was Prefect of Studies 1940-44 before returning to the United States.

Not knowing when they all got back from Rome to London what the future had in store, Fr. Dyson had made a point of shaking hands with each member of the large group of English seminarians and wishing them good luck. Before his arrival at the Gregorian Scripture studies there had been regarded as particularly poor. Storey felt exceedingly lucky to be taught by him and was careful to explain why.

I enjoyed particularly the lectures of our Jesuit Father Dyson, who was a great scriptural expert....I'd always been fascinated with evolution....[by] the fossils we used to find at Whitby, especially in the cliffs. I found it difficult when there was this great controversy, with Catholics being against Huxley and against the whole of the Darwinian theory about evolution. Dyson was brilliant and he helped us to recognise that actually the whole of the bible writing about that was portraying God as a good workman who does a good week's job and rests. And so he fits it into the six days, the first three being the separation of light and dark and earth and water and land and sky; and then the second three days fitting them up with things, and it is actually evolutionary….and evolution moves up right to man at the very end….The whole thing is an evolution, a process and I do remember that about our scripture studies and our studies of the later biblical books. It's deplorable how little most Catholic priests studied scripture. I don't know whether it's any better now, but it was very bad….Bob Dyson….taught us so much about the psalms and the book of Job, which is such an important book and….I do remember that with very great gratitude.

At last Storey's mind was fully engaged, riding the crest of a wave of fresh knowledge and understanding. Under Fr. Dyson's tutelage a conviction was nurtured of the importance of reading texts fully for oneself instead of falling back on commentaries, advice later strongly re-inforced at Cambridge. It was no use talking about writers without having read them.

During his pre-ordination year Storey became the College's Senior Student, the key point of liaison between the superiors and the student body, and someone both trusted and respected. If there had been serious doubts about his attitude and outlook during his early years in Rome, by this stage they had long been dispelled. Intellectually and in other ways the period leading up to his ordination was exciting and satisfying. These last years of study for the priesthood were also 'a very mysterious and frightening time….we really were not sure whether Germany was going to defeat us….or whether we were going to win'. And yet, whether or not the war was won, a cast-iron conviction as to his future direction continued to elude him.

As with philosophy, his theological studies were divided into two parts, firstly a baccalaureate and then a licentiate. He was one of a group of nine at St. Mary's Hall who were examined for the former by Fathers Leeming and Dyson and a Fr. George Ekbery in the summer of 1941. Compared with groups both before and after, they performed outstandingly. The grading system at the Gregorian was (and remains) on a 10 point scale, with a pass mark (or probatus) of 6.0 to 6.5. Two of Storey's colleagues were awarded the highest possible mark of 10 (*summa cum laude*). The remainder, including Storey, were awarded a 9 (*magna cum laude*). Individually and collectively, it was an outstanding performance. The results for the licentiate examinations two years later, however, were very different. Three of them (including one of those with a mark of 10 for the baccalaureate) failed, with marks of 4 or 5. There was one 9.5, one 9, two 7.5s, and Storey with a bare pass of 6. Given his very positive remarks about how much he had enjoyed his work in theology, this result is puzzling: on the other hand, in view of his criticism of teaching at the Gregorian, standards there were evidently lower than at St. Mary's. There is a twist to the tale. The formal certificate recording Storey's achievement of a Licentiate in Sacred Theology is dated Rome, 24 April 1950, and this gives his grade as *bene probatus* or between 6.6 and 7.5 on the marking scale. The delay in formal certification was no doubt due to the difficulties associated with wartime and the slow return to normal arrangements thereafter. Furthermore, as part of the strict conditions governing arrangements between St. Mary's Hall and the Gregorian, there may have been procedures whereby the original marks were moderated by external examiners, as in secular universities. It would appear that Storey, and no doubt some of his colleagues, benefited from some such arrangement.

Progress towards ordination was phased but inexorable. Storey had been tonsured in 'a freezing but very well performed ceremony at the Leonine College' on 21 January 1940, five months before his repatriation from Rome. William Godfrey, now Archbishop and Apostolic Delegate in Britain, presided over the

17: Stonyhurst: Ordination Group, 14 February 1943
(Storey back row, far left)

services, both held in the Chapel at St. Mary's Hall, during which Storey received his first and second minor orders on 1 December 1940 and 7 June 1941. He was ordained Sub-Deacon at St. Mary's by Bishop Griffin, then Auxiliary Bishop of Birmingham, on 30 May 1942; and Deacon, also at St. Mary's, by Bishop Marshall of Salford. His ordination as a Priest was also scheduled to be presided over by Bishop Marshall in the Chapel of St. Aloysius (the Boys' Chapel) at Stonyhurst on 14 February 1943.

The precise circumstances in which he finally determined to proceed to priestly ordination are best described by himself.

I remember still being doubtful because so many of my friends had left by now and joined up and not a few of them had been killed, and was I to continue?...It was the last week's retreat and preparation for ordination and the priest giving the retreat [was] Agnellus Andrew, who eventually became head of BBC religious broadcasting. And I thought I'd ask him a question which had nothing to do with religion….and if he answered the question in the affirmative it meant I should go on, and if in the negative that I shouldn't. I'd been asking God for some sign but hadn't any certainty….I went into him in my turn….and almost as soon as he greeted me he said: 'Ah, Tony, come in, I think you have a question for me' and he recounted the question and said: 'The answer is I think yes', and it was just fantastic.

With that extraordinary episode what had previously been less than entirely positive feelings were dispelled. Lingering doubts were rendered redundant. From then onwards he 'never had any doubt whatever that that is what the Lord wanted me to be'. He now knew that the incident with the Mill Hill Father at Bishop's Court had been an authentic sign. Later, following the anxious discussions with his parents and siblings, his clear decision to test his vocation had been the right one. The contretemps at the English College had been survived. Years later he recalled that it was on the day of his ordination that the Russians had captured Rostov from the retreating Germans; and during that week Beveridge's Social Services bill had passed its first reading in the House of Commons. 'My own pastoral hopes were touched by this [because] I was looking forward to parish work': the effect of his seminary training was to whet his appetite for life as a pastor..

He said his first Mass in the Boys' Chapel at Stonyhurst and his second near the family home, in the church of SS. Mary and Everilda on the estate at Everingham. His ordination brought great joy to his entire family.

Four months later they were plunged into grief. Storey's eldest brother, Gerard, had joined the Royal Air Force on a short-service commission before the war and spent some time training pilots in Iraq. At the outbreak of hostilities he returned to Britain and by 1943 was regularly flying sorties over Germany. In June that year, on a bombing mission over Cologne, his plane was shot down. There were no survivors. George Storey never fully recovered from the shock of this bereavement. He retired from his post at Everingham and he and Harriet went to live nearby in an old rectory at Harswell. Family life for all of them was never the same again.

CHAPTER FOUR
CHRIST'S COLLEGE, CAMBRIDGE

We do not know when Storey learned of what was next in store for him. Thomas Shine, Bishop of Middlesbrough, asked him to undertake a degree in History at Cambridge. A year earlier another young priest from the diocese, Fr. Patrick McEnroe, had been sent to Oxford to read English. According to Storey – though there is no documentary evidence of this - the reason for these decisions was a scheme for the dioceses of Leeds and Middlesbrough to collaborate in establishing a secondary school in the York area.

A notable achievement amidst the many difficulties of the inter-war period was a plan for a major re-organisation of the national system of schooling. The Hadow Report of 1926 recommended that all children compulsorily transfer at the age of eleven to a distinct system of secondary education. Together with the Spens Report of 1938, this formed the basis of the wartime coalition government's Education Act of 1944 which provided secondary education for all up to the age of fifteen. Subsequently, Catholic education was a major beneficiary. An immediate reaction in Catholic circles was that the legislation would require a substantial increase in the number of priests who were also teachers.

Storey maintained that the question of the school's location eventually provoked an irreconcilable difference between the dioceses. The school never materialised and after completing their degrees he and Fr. McEnroe were assigned to parochial duties in Middlesbrough. Meanwhile, they benefited from, and in both cases greatly enjoyed, an entirely unexpected bonus. Few priests in either diocese, or in any other for that matter, had been educated at University. Previously, most of those who proceeded to that level had graduated in either Philosophy or Theology. To be given the opportunity of studying some other subject at University was rare until the advent of the new policy for secondary education.

While in Cambridge he stayed at St. Edmund's House which, along with the Benedictine Benet House, was where most Catholic clergy lived during their studies. Neither establishment was a College and could not, therefore, matriculate (enrol) students in the University. Students staying there had to be affiliated to a College, and for both St. Edmund's and Benet House that College was always Christ's. No time was lost in approaching the University. The single-sheet application form, which Storey completed and sent to S.W. Grose, Senior Tutor of Christ's College, is not dated. Fr. John Petit, Master of St. Edmund's, wrote a very brief letter to Grose on 10 March, seeking a place for Storey from the forthcoming Michaelmas term, saying that he 'comes well-recommended'. This was followed by a single-sentence missive of 15 March from Monsignor John Macmillan, still Rector of St. Mary's Hall. He confirmed that the applicant, whom he had known for five years (and whose ordination he had witnessed a month earlier), was 'of good moral character'. Storey was formally noted in the College Admissions Book among the next batch of prospective students to be matriculated on 19 April 1943.

Several factors coalesced in this remarkably truncated admissions procedure. A close relationship had developed between St. Edmund's House and Christ's College since the time of John Peile, Master of the College around the turn of the 19th century; this was also true of Benet House, most of whose students were from religious orders, which was then located within the Christ's College grounds. Secondly, following the wartime introduction of conscription for men aged 20 or more, most Colleges were only 'rather more than half full', so competition for places was weak or non-existent. Also, and perhaps primarily, there was little need to scrutinize the academic credentials of someone who already held two qualifications from the Gregorian University. Storey was admitted without fuss. Several other Catholic priests became members of Christ's College during the early 1940s, including his contemporary at the English College, now also recently ordained (for the archdiocese of Liverpool), Fr. Joseph Holland, who matriculated on 29 April 1943 for the following Michaelmas term. Apparently, Storey had no formal responsibilities to discharge between his ordination and the commencement of his studies in Cambridge. After a long break, much of it perhaps spent with his grieving family in Everingham, he registered as one of 59 undergraduates at Christ's College in the early autumn of 1943.

St. Edmund's House, founded in 1896, had been financed by the 15th Duke of Norfolk to enable Catholic clergy, particularly secular clergy, to study at the University. The buildings had formerly been a hall for training evangelical Anglican clergy, and Norfolk bought the property through an agent, fearing that the owners might refuse to sell for purposes of establishing a Catholic house of studies. For many years student numbers were tiny and St. Edmund's often teetered on the brink of unviability. However, this situation altered dramatically once the new Education Act was in prospect. The number of priests in residence reached a peak of 36 (24 of them seculars) during 1944-45, the last year of the war and the middle year of Storey's time there.

During the previous decade the buildings and facilities at St. Edmund's had been enlarged and improved. Nevertheless, in

October 1944 Fr. Petit reported that the House was bursting at the seams with students. To meet their needs there were only five bathrooms, seven W.C.s, and nine altars in the Chapel where residents could say morning Mass. In his view the House was 'not just full, but overfull'. Besides the Chapel, there was a dining room, a library and a combination (or common) room, and Storey had his own bed-sitting-room-cum study. Compared with its situation only a short time earlier, St. Edmund's was now prosperous, diverse and lively. As befitted a residential institution for ordained men, discipline was fairly relaxed, to the point where some bishops felt it was too liberal. However, in pursuit of an enhanced reputation for the House, the Master was keen for residents to be free to participate as fully as possible in activities in the rest of the University. This attitude fitted precisely with Storey's own approach to his new way of life. He arrived with two ambitions, neither of which, however, he was ultimately able to fulfil: to achieve a First-Class degree and to win a Blue for rugby.

He was glad to resume his rugby career at a seriously competitive level, playing at fly-half throughout his years at Cambridge and enjoying it 'tremendously'. The official records of the Christ's College Rugby Football Club are not extant for this period, so we have to fall back on the sparser material in the College *Magazine*. The depleted University numbers of the early war years made it impossible for some Colleges, including Christ's, to field a full team, in Christ's case obliging them to join with Sidney Sussex College. This ended as Storey arrived in 1943 'owing to the increasing keenness of everyone concerned'. Unfortunately, four of their league matches during the Michaelmas term were cancelled, but they managed to win all but one of their remaining fixtures. Matters deteriorated again in the Lent term when there were barely sufficient players to make a team. However, the College participated strongly in the

'Cuppers', the inter-collegiate knockout competition, and for the first time reached the finals where, having lost a player (possibly Storey) through injury, they were narrowly defeated 6 - 3 by Trinity Hall. There is no mention of Storey in any of the reports for 1943-44. Yet in the Michaelmas term of the following year, i.e. at the beginning of his second year, Storey was one of four students to be awarded his College's Colours for rugby. For this to have happened it is highly likely that he had played well in several games for the First XV during the previous season; and, injuries apart, he played regularly for the College thereafter.

In Storey's final academic year, 1945-46, he was elected Captain of the Christ College First XV. That year's intake to the College included no fewer than 68 ex-servicemen, among them Capt. Charles Reidy, a married man who had also been educated and played rugby at Stonyhurst, though before Storey's time. Reidy was one of four brothers who had played for the London Irish club during the 1930s and as a second-row forward he had won a cap for Ireland versus Wales in Belfast in 1936-37. During the war he served with the 2nd Battalion, the London Irish Rifles, in North Africa, was severely wounded, and enrolled at Christ's College as part of a rehabilitative transfer to the Army Education Corps. He had already been influential in developing the sport of hammer-throwing, building the first stone circle in 1943, and went on to success in the sport, as well as winning a University half-blue for throwing the discus. As soon as he arrived Reidy was appointed coach and Vice-President of the Christ's College Rugby Club; and, as Captain and with five others, Storey joined him on the Committee. The two men became close friends: apart from their time on the rugby field, they both enjoyed debating and often walked to lectures together. They and their colleagues, however, met with mixed success on the field of play.

The College *Magazine* summarized their season as follows:

The [Michaelmas] term was not as successful as we had

18: Christ's College, Cambridge: 1st XV with Storey as Captain in the centre of the middle row, and his friend and the Coach, Capt. Charles Reidy, on his left.

hoped, for we lost nine out of the eleven games, though mostly by narrow margins. The forwards improved considerably under the coaching of C.J. Reidy, but the backs lacked the necessary pace. However, in the Lent Term our efforts were rewarded, and of the six matches played, four were won....In the Cuppers we began with a win against Peterhouse (30-3) but were beaten by Trinity (0-9) in the second round after a close game.

At some point in his Cambridge rugby career Storey suffered a serious knee injury and 'ended up in Addenbrooke's Hospital for quite a long time'. There he was embarrassed and ashamed – 'so little one was doing for the war'- to find himself in the midst of numerous severely wounded and disabled American servicemen, who 'were absolute heroes'.

He also enjoyed playing cricket at Cambridge, though there is no trace of this in the College records, so his involvement in the sport was probably merely recreational. As someone who had spent much of his younger days in the saddle, he sometimes went to Newmarket for the races. And it was there in June 1945, just after the war had ended, that he was a partisan member of the crowd of 30,000 which saw 'Dante' win the Derby. With so many other racecourses devoted to military purposes (principally demobilisation at that stage) the Derby was run at Newmarket that year. Widely known as 'The Idol of the North' and bred at Middleham in the North Riding, 'Dante' won by two lengths, whereupon there 'was great rejoicing in Yorkshire' and no doubt in St. Edmund's House too.

Indoors at the College Storey returned to debating. Over three centuries earlier John Milton had been a member of Christ's and it was the Milton Society which organised College debates. Storey became a regular and leading member of the Society. His debut came during his second term at Christ's, in February 1944, when he joined Fr. Joe Holland in proposing the motion (which was subsequently carried) that 'Religious Education is not the business of the State School'. Between then and June 1946 he spoke in a further ten debates, often as a lead speaker for or against a motion, but also from the floor. While it is unwise to read too much into raw statistics, his advocacy appears to have been effective, for he was on the losing side only once during the eleven debates. He certainly enjoyed the confidence of his colleagues. In March 1945 he was elected as the '5th person' to join the President, Vice-President, Secretary and Deputy-Secretary in running the Society. In May 1945 (possibly when he was in Addenbrooke's Hospital recovering from his injury) he asked to be relieved, but was elected again in March 1946.

Five of his eleven speeches were about religion, ethics or, specifically, Christianity: the rest were about other matters. In October 1944 he was the lead proposer of the motion: 'In a benevolent despotism lies the only hope for our civilisation'.

The grapes of democracy really were sour. It would not work without at least a common end in view. Its politics were colourless, there was no stability....politicians had lost the idea of service to the community. The necessities of life....were domestic liberties, religious freedom, and good law. Government was an expert job, and only a few could know its intricacies....Most people did not mind who governed them, as long as they were well looked after.... Despots....would not oppress people if there was nothing to be gained by it, and there would not be disorder if they ruled for the benefit of the world, and not only one nation.

This contribution suggests that, while his interests had broadened and his intellect had sharpened at St. Mary's, his views, perhaps particularly those aired publicly, were those of a conservative Catholic priest.

Society was a natural hierarchy; some kind of coercion was needed, and obedience to a lawful authority was a virtue. The Church itself was a despotism.

Unsurprisingly, in the era of Hitler, Stalin and Mussolini, the motion was heavily defeated.

His successful contributions were invariably analytical, working from first principles, and in structure appear to have owed a good deal both to his work for the Higher Religious Certificate and his study of Philosophy. In February 1945, for instance, he proposed that 'satisfactory moral standards depend on belief in God'. Defining morals as the science of human behaviour, he asked how could man set a moral standard without belief in God.

For a man to be moral his mind, will and appetite must be in harmony and the man must aim at prudence, fortitude, temperance and justice....This broke down....every man would judge in his own case, and this would be

88

unsatisfactory as the man could lower his moral standard to suit the occasion; and anyhow, if everyone had a different standard of morality, it might be a little difficult….an authority was required to set that standard.

He was content to face hostility, 'staggering the House' in December 1944 'by claiming that God's existence can be proved by reason'. On the other hand, of all the clerical debaters - and there were several at Christ's College in his time besides himself and Fr. Holland – he was the least likely to purvey a purely clerical line. And if his style of speaking at this stage developed towards that of his more mature years, it was above all rational, conversational and far from strident.

In one of his last contributions in May 1946, in a debate on a motion requesting the United Nations to depose the current Spanish regime (when his friend, Charles Reidy, was also a speaker), Storey gave his current view of a country whose affairs had interested him deeply for a decade.

> Fr. Storey deplored the lack of liberty in Spain, but considered that any interference would cause much more hardship to the common people and would therefore not be justified.

In closing the proceedings, the President commended the speakers on the high standard of their performance. It appears that in this arena and on the rugby field Storey made a valuable contribution to undergraduate life at Christ's College which he also hugely enjoyed.

Beyond the University, Storey was called upon regularly at weekends to undertake pastoral duties. Most of these involved travelling to prisoner-of-war camps to say Mass for Germans or Italians; or likewise for Americans on one of the many U.S. air bases in East Anglia. When visiting American bases he had the use of a car. Otherwise, like most students in Cambridge, he went all over the city on a bicycle; and this was also how he usually got out of the city into the surrounding fenlands. Once there, he could indulge his lifelong love of walking.

> [In Cambridgeshire] walking in the country was wonderful - Madingley woods. I remember lying in the woods and hearing a couple of nightingales singing together. That was an absolutely fantastic experience.

During the last year of the war he and a friend cycled all the way through Mildenhall to Walsingham 'to pay....our respects to Our Lady'. With American bombers flying out eastwards and doodlebugs coming in from the west they slept for a while in a haystack; and then:

> in the middle of this dark forest in the brecklands there was a nightingale singing; we actually heard it sing through midnight. A great memory. We got to Walsingham the next morning and were just about asleep.

In Cambridge itself he had vivid memories of great American tank carriers rumbling through the city during the build-up to D-Day. 'We knew something was happening: everybody was moving south'.

Storey worked hard academically. Wartime attitudes towards study, where they were positive – and some, understandably, were not – were also unremittingly serious. He was urged to read as widely as possible; he had to present an essay at least every fortnight; and together with his teachers and fellow students the issues which emerged from their work were discussed 'with great urgency'. Even when on vacation there was lots of reading to be done and essays to be written. Like many mothers before and since, Harriet Storey did not regard reading and writing as work and, in order to progress, he was often obliged to retreat to a private room in a nearby convent. The demands of war had revived the country's agriculture and, with his father ailing, there was always plenty to do on the farm; and not only there, because much other ground, previously spare or used for other purposes such as lawns and tennis courts, was now cultivated. During one summer Storey joined a neighbour in scything an entire field of oats. Rationing was widespread but those who lived rurally fared best. Harriet would send him out to shoot a rabbit or a mallard and by that stage of the war they could get both meat and grain without too much difficulty; and, of course, 'the odd thing would fall off the back of a wagon'. Whether he was in Cambridge or Everingham, life, though safe, was busy.

Storey's academic record at Cambridge may be briefly summarised. He won no prizes, exhibitions or scholarships, almost certainly not competing for them. In each of his three sets of examinations for the History Tripos – Preliminaries in June 1944, Part I in June 1945, and Part II in June 1946 – he was placed in the Second Class, Upper Division. He graduated B.A. on 22 June 1946 and proceeded to the formality of an M.A. in 1950 - within the shortest prescribed period, i.e. six years from the end of his first term of residence. Thus, he was not only successful but, unlike his experience as a seminarian, uniformly so. Yet, as with many other students, the value of his time at University was much greater than is suggested by the bald facts of his academic record.

Although his course had been chosen for him, he greatly enjoyed his work, which had certainly not been the case in Rome.

I found the course at Cambridge absolutely fascinating. It was completely explosive to my mind and totally liberating from the [previous] kind of learning. At last I met scholarship.

His programme involved the study of European history from the fall of the Roman Empire to the 17th century. This range of material admirably complemented and further developed his previous work in philosophy and theology. In addition to opening up new vistas of knowledge, it provided valuable contextual background and enhanced his appreciation and understanding of both subjects. A background of world war also provided a unique perspective.

Studying European history….while the whole world was at war was like watching a film going past at speed and bringing it right up to date. It was an extraordinary experience and I found it really exhilarating….[It] affected me theologically because my subject really was the foundation….and development of Europe….starting off with the barbarian invasions and where we'd all come from and how we'd swept across the world.

Right from the start of his studies he was strongly encouraged to read the work of a host of great thinkers and writers; and he had at his disposal the library facilities and, crucially, the time to do so.

The extraordinary thing I found about Cambridge was [that]…. if you were going to deal with Martin Luther, then *read* the man. If you were going to deal with Wycliffe, then read his writing. If you were going to deal with Plato, then read *The Republic.* If you were going to deal with Marxism, then read the *Manifesto* and *Das Kapital*….that openness to what people were doing at different times was quite staggering really and I was so grateful.

In ranging far beyond the boundaries of the syllabus of his course, he became an avid reader; and, as long as his eyesight permitted, he remained one for the rest of his life.

There were difficulties. Later, when he looked back to the Church's attitudes at that time he found them 'extremely illiberal'. The index of prohibited books had caused problems in

Rome and continued to do so. 'I wasn't allowed to read half the stuff for my set reading when I got to Cambridge.' While we do not know whether or not he stuck to these rules, against this background he found it 'enlightening' to be taught by 'people who had no axe to grind'. In Storey's time, however, that could not be said of at least one Cambridge academic: Professor G.C. Coulton, an ardent Protestant low-churchman who was both a leading medievalist and a keen anti-Catholic controversialist, and who had devoted much of his career to refuting the historical writings of Cardinal Adrian Gasquet. A Fellow of St. John's College and by then well into his eighties, he had continued to lecture because so many other historians were absent fighting or on war work, but was now about to retire. Arriving slightly late to listen to one of Coulton's last lectures and being unfamiliar with the venue, Storey entered the hall by the wrong door; and, in front of a packed audience but unseen by the lecturer, perched himself underneath the table from which Coulton was speaking. In due course and in ascending order of gravity, the three great evils which still needed to be confronted were vigorously denounced: Nazism, Communism and – with the speaker thumping the table above Storey, who was in clerical attire – Roman Catholicism. Aware of their lecturer's reputation as a hater of Catholics, the other students had seen the funny side of this situation for some time. Finally, and sadly to Coulton's bewilderment, they burst into uncontrolled laughter.

If this incident was untoward but fleeting, another encounter was of benign and lasting significance. It was Storey's great good fortune at Cambridge to have as one of his teachers Dom David Knowles, the outstanding English medievalist of the 20th century. Knowles enjoyed a stellar career at Cambridge, becoming Professor of Medieval History in 1947, just after Storey's time, and then Regius Professor of Modern History in 1954 until his retirement in 1963. Having studied for his first degree (a double

First in Philosophy and Classics, with a Distinction in Philosophy) at Christ's College, he was successively a member of the Benedictine communities at Downside and then, having been required to move by his Abbot following a disagreement, at Ealing Abbey. This disagreement about the future development of Downside – whether it should continue with its substantial parish work and increasingly heavy engagement in building up the School, or whether a group led by Dom David should break off to form a more contemplative alternative elsewhere – persuaded him to leave Ealing in 1939, leading automatically to his suspension from the order and to his being forbidden to say Mass or receive the sacrament. After some years this was rectified through a formal process of exclaustration whereby his priestly functions were restored: though he was under no obligation to return to Downside or Ealing, he remained a faithful monk to the end of his life.

Much of this long post-dated Storey's encounter with him. While some students wondered about Knowles's ecclesiastical status, few knew the details and the consensus is that they in no way disturbed their relations with him as a teacher. It was in 1944, at the start of Storey's second year at Cambridge, that Dom Knowles was appointed to a Teaching Fellowship at Peterhouse College, and a year later to a University Lectureship. Knowles' special interest was in the history of English monasticism, and he produced major, definitive works on the subject. Having imbibed much from his father, Storey was able greatly to extend his knowledge and understanding of northern monasticism. In particular, Knowles introduced him to the writings of Aelred, for two decades from 1147 Abbot of the Cistercian Abbey at Rievaulx in north Yorkshire. Under Knowles he 'made a great study' of Aelred – probably his major undergraduate project - reading many of his sermons and translating some of them. Above all, he encountered Aelred's treatise 'On Spiritual

Friendship'. It was at this point that Storey's academic work and his personal life came into close and permanent conjunction.

Aelred's treatise was a synthesis of his Classical education and the Cistercian tradition. It was originally inspired by his reading of Cicero 'On Friendship' as a young man, but was largely written and completed only towards the end of his life. Its structure was that of a dialogue between himself and three other monks, which for Storey immediately underlined the importance of others in the development of a spiritual life. Together Aelred and his younger colleagues identified different levels of friendship, the lowest being a relationship of sensual pleasure. One based on temporal advantage and possessions was of a higher order. That based on Christ's commandment to love was the highest of all. This might blossom into a spiritual friendship attained through conforming to Christ by wholesale interaction between two people without thought of gain. The relationship built up both parties and helped them journey towards God. Storey recognised that the treatise challenged many modern and conventional concepts of the spiritual life. According to Aelred, that life was not simply about 'me and God' to the exclusion of others. Spiritual growth was unattainable if individuals did not develop in the manner in which they related to others. Yet, in contrast, Storey recalled that:

> you weren't….allowed to have special friendships with boys at College in your training….I don't know why really, I suppose it was the homosexual thing….particular friendships were dangerous. You must always sit in a different chair, in a different room, the common room or wherever you are….Aelred….taught….how important it was to have particular friendships and also how important it was to make sure they were kept in balance, kept in order. There was this abbot, writing in the twelfth century about [the] community life of men of the same sex and in a sense

almost quietly aware of the dangers, but also aware of the importance of having a faithful, trusting relationship with somebody else.

Storey subsequently applied Aelred's teaching to his relations with both sexes and regarded his encounter with the treatise as one of the intellectual and emotional turning-points in his life. It persuaded him to set aside some of the precepts urged on him earlier. In this sphere in particular, he decided to trust his own instincts and, where he judged it appropriate, to take an independent line. His attitude towards relationships and towards counselling others in their regard was never the same again. He moved on decisively.

Storey was exceedingly fortunate to have encountered Knowles in this way. Professors were not involved in tutoring undergraduates and Dom David was elected to a chair in 1947. So, the only two academic sessions in which they could have come together in the way that they did were 1944-45 and 1945-46. While Storey was undoubtedly a major beneficiary of their interaction, his tutor thought highly of him and encouraged him to stay on at Cambridge to conduct research. This was never part of Storey's plan but, if he had done so, he would have looked further at the Cistercians. Nor is there much doubt that David Knowles benefited from the relationship. At that very early stage in his Cambridge career, he was still winning acceptance at Peterhouse, but only slowly, partly on account of his Catholicism, and partly because he was known to be at odds with his superiors. He would have relished introducing a young priest to Aelred and his writings.

As he approached the end of his course and prepared to take up his first diocesan duties back in Yorkshire, something else had a marked influence on Storey. Particularly during his period in Rome, he had become uncomfortably aware of how illiberal official Church attitudes had become during the later 19th and early 20th centuries, with 'strong prohibitions all over the place'. In addition, the only discernible role for the laity in the life of the Church was an exceedingly quiescent one: 'the Church....was just the Pope and the bishops and the priests. The laity did nothing really and had nothing'. He had welcomed the first signs of change in all this at Stonyhurst with the development of the notion of Catholic Action under Pius XI. Then what he came to regard as a major step in the right direction emerged just a few months after his ordination, with Pius XII's encyclical *Mystici Corporis.* While this was published virtually unnoticed during the war, its significance became much clearer as people set about rebuilding their lives in peacetime. The encyclical was grounded in the theological notion, developed during the 1920s and 1930s, of the Church as the Mystical Body of Christ: body because it was a living entity; of Christ because He was its Head; and mystical because the Church was neither purely physical nor purely spiritual, but supernatural. The encyclical contained clear denunciations of several recent evils – discrimination on the basis of race or nationality, the murder of disabled people, and the forced conversion of others. Its central thrust, however, was to include the laity as equal and important elements in the body of Christ. They were in the front line of Church life and should be conscious not merely of belonging to the Church, but of *being* the Church. This argument was to be developed much further in *Lumen Gentium,* one of the seminal documents of the Second Vatican Council. Meanwhile, he was enthused by the encyclical, which formed a welcome backdrop to the start of his work in the diocese of Middlesbrough.

Storey's student days in Cambridge had a profound and permanent influence on him. They encapsulated a prolonged process of intellectual awakening during a period when he had the time and other resources to respond to its urgings. For three years he listened avidly, read voraciously and, in discussing and debating, honed the skills as a communicator for which he eventually became renowned. In David Knowles he encountered the embodiment of the happy co-existence of deep faith and deep scholarship. And in studying the writings of Aelred of Rievaulx he discovered what came to constitute one of the wellsprings of his entire approach to life. Moreover, as he turned to the reality of parochial work, there were signs, albeit at first almost imperceptible, that the Church was moving in a more positive direction.

CHAPTER FIVE

MIDDLESBROUGH AND SALTBURN
1946-55

After investing in Storey's training for a decade Bishop Shine decided to throw him in at the deep end of parochial life. As soon as he got back to Yorkshire Storey was sent as Curate, not to some quiet rural parish of the kind to which his family had belonged in Pocklington, but to a tough location - the parish of St. Joseph's on the Grove Hill estate in Middlesbrough. Few postings were further removed from the ordered, scholarly atmosphere of St. Edmund's House and Christ's College, Cambridge. It was a 'complete new world' and Storey took to it like a duck to water. 'I had never done any parish work and hadn't any idea what it might be like; and so it was quite an excitement'. In a deprived area at a difficult time, his work was arduous and often stressful. He made mistakes and had some frightening experiences. On the other hand he was well received, relished the variety, and what happened to him was of lasting influence.

In mid-1946 Britain was still in the earliest stages of recovery from the war. The country was hugely indebted and unable to function economically without massive American aid. Demobilisation was far from complete, rationing was more severe than during the war, and many communities faced the task of repairing damage inflicted by bombardment. A centre of the steel industry and later a supplier of munitions and Mulberry harbours, Middlesbrough had been the first major British town to be bombed, in May 1940, though damage overall was less than elsewhere. There was, however, a substantial legacy of neglect from earlier times. Industrial development was late in coming to Teesside but, after the discovery in 1850 of ironstone in the nearby Eston hills, it proceeded very rapidly indeed. A population of 7,600 in 1851 grew to 90,000 by 1900, with a large preponderance of males over females and many immigrants, particularly from Ireland – leading one commentator to recognise features 'generally credited only to the towns of the American West'. While population continued to grow, the economy slumped after the First World War and the town suffered very high rates of unemployment and distress between the wars. Conditions in the town centre, which was grossly overcrowded and had some of the worst housing in the country, deteriorated rapidly. Grove Hill, on the outskirts, was among the first of the new estates to be developed by the Corporation during the 1920s as it tried to provide affordable housing for ordinary people, but work there was far from complete when Storey arrived.

In terms of membership and personnel the situation of Catholicism in the diocese was promising. No new churches or schools had been built during the war, but Middlesbrough had more Catholics than any other town in England except Preston. The diocese had 55,000 Catholics in 1929 and 96,000 in 1955; simultaneously diocesan priests rose from 86 to 140, and parish churches from 45 to 74. Although conditions were challenging, Storey had joined a rapidly expanding organisation.

He knew his fellow Curate, Fr. Paddy McEnroe, very well indeed. Paddy's parents had moved to England from Ireland when he was a youngster, he had been a year ahead of Storey at the English College and St. Mary's Hall, and was back from Oxford. The Parish Priest was Canon James McMullan, a craggy Glaswegian in his mid-fifties. The new estates had been located at some distance from existing churches, and from 1925 McMullan and other priests from the Cathedral had gone out to say Mass in a tin hut at Grove Hill. A parish had been established under Fr. George Kiernan in 1926, with the then Fr. McMullan succeeding him in 1931 and presiding there, ultimately as a Monsignor, till his death in 1969. A parish church and a primary school had been completed before the war, on rough land still littered with gorse and infested with rabbits, and there was also a presbytery and a small men's club.

McMullan came straight to the point on first meeting his new curates. 'So you have a degree from Cambridge', he said to Storey; and to Paddy McEnroe, 'and you have a degree from Oxford'. 'Yes, Father', they replied. 'Then you'll have no difficulty selling these raffle tickets'! Some priority had to be given to finance. Annual income was just over £2,000. The proceeds of various social activities (no doubt including raffles), and of a 1,000 members' club and an annual garden fete were devoted to clearing debts, the largest of which, at £8,380, was for the church. Out of a general population of some 25,000, some 4,000 were Catholics and most of them were poor. Some were among the squatters in Nissen huts and unfinished or previously empty houses, most without electricity, and many were unemployed. Competitors for jobs included people from the town centre and members of the Polish land army encamped on the moors to the south. Following the Education Act of 1944 and with the gradual implementation of the Beveridge Report, there were hopes of better times to come: but against a background of defeated Fascism and spreading Communism, 'we were not too sure', according to Storey, 'whether or not....state interference was going to be a good thing'.

He had boundless energy and great goodwill, but also a somewhat formal demeanour and an upper-crust accent (though for purposes of humour he readily slipped into east Yorkshire dialect). He was enormously gratified, therefore, to receive a warm welcome from parishioners.

19: St. Joseph's Church on the Grove Hill Estate in Middlesbrough.

Apart from church services....our job....was to visit the people and get to know them and try to help them where we could. What amazed me was how welcome one was as a priest....and when you came to a house you'd always be taken into the front room, which was the posh one kept for visitors, until you got to know the family well and then you'd be more readily acceptable in the kitchen. And often too when you knocked on the door they'd say: 'What are you knocking for? The door's open'. Everybody's door was open in those days; you'd take it for granted that the priest could just walk into the house without saying anything. I was very impressed with the love that people showed us and very quickly I began to find a great affection for them. So many people were new to the area, having just come back from the war, as I was new to the area, and they left very deep impressions upon me.

He had safely crossed a social divide, and was probably more relieved than he cared to admit. He also found that he loved working among poor, deprived and uneducated people, and that he and they found it easy to grow fond of each other.

Fr. Peter Keeling, who presided at Storey's funeral and whose family lived on the Grove Hill estate in the 1940s, had other tales to tell besides the one about raffle tickets: how Storey paid for Peter's father, an unemployed steel worker, to attend a retreat which he had organised in Sunderland; how he joined and energised local meetings of the Young Christian Worker movement, then very active in Middlesbrough; and how, when one of their neighbours, Mrs. Savage, fell ill, Storey went round each morning before saying Mass to lay and light her fire. 'He became a legend not only in my family but far and wide for this sort of generosity, compassion and sensitivity'. There is more than a suggestion here of a deliberate reaching out to the sort of individuals with whom hitherto he had had no dealings. Years later he loved walking in the countryside with groups of his parishioners, but it was from this point, in Middlesbrough, that he began generally to enjoy doing ordinary things with ordinary people. His priesthood became securely anchored in caring for those he was called to serve; and because their circumstances were utterly different from those he had previously experienced, he was alive to their needs.

Storey also helped to breathe fresh life into the parish youth club, which catered for both sexes, and whose activities the curates divided between them. Looking after the boys, he formed a cricket team and encouraged the football and rugby teams. The youth club had a very good football team, coached by one of the goalkeepers from Middlesbrough F.C., which one year won the final of the Under 18s competition, playing the match at Middlesbrough's ground at Ayresome Park. Storey himself played cricket for a local league side. Raising money for Nazareth House, a diocesan children's home, he also turned out at football as goalkeeper for a team of Catholic clergy in an annual fixture against the local police: being primarily a rugby player, he had to be warned against tackling opposing forwards bearing down on his goal! Most unusually as a cleric, he also played rugby for Middlesbrough (being offered, but turning down, a trial for Yorkshire). His continuing active involvement in his favourite sport on Saturdays meant that he sometimes appeared at Mass on Sundays with a black eye, a limp or an arm in a sling.

His efforts were neither straightforward nor always successful. Paddy McEnroe worked with him only briefly, soon being posted as Curate to St. Charles's in Hull, but they shared at least one intimidating experience in Middlesbrough. One of their duties was to visit families who, for whatever reason, no longer practised the faith. Paddy returned from one encounter lamenting that he had been kicked out of the house by a big, strong man, a blacksmith: he 'wouldn't have anything to do with the Holy God stuff'. Being taller and sturdier than Paddy, Storey decided to 'have a go….because we were both recently ordained and had that zest that one has'. So a day or two later, in black suit and clerical collar, he visited the blacksmith who, with 'Oh! another of you….picked me up as though I was made of feather weight and threw me over his privet hedge into the next door garden'. While Paddy 'howled with laughter', Storey chalked it up as 'one of those happy memories of realising that not everyone is in love with the Lord, or at least with the institution of the Lord'.

20: Canon James McMullan

There were other hazards. One night Fr. McMullan got back to the presbytery after Storey had gone to bed. He was furious, having had a row with the Secretary of the Men's Club, and called Storey downstairs to discuss it over a drink. In those early post-war days alcohol was scarce, though it was usually possible to get gin and some very cheap, sweet wine which, when mixed, was known as 'gin and odd'. When parish priests retailed their woes curates were expected to listen, but by the time Storey had downed three hefty glasses of this tipple he was far from steady on his feet. Leaving McMullan still mumbling at the kitchen table, he crawled upstairs. When he failed to appear to say the parish Mass next morning, the housekeeper found him slumped against his bed. Mass was a little late and not 'a very prayerful occasion', but the parishioners were content, having been told by the housekeeper that Storey 'was so holy and [had] never even gone to bed..[but]..fallen asleep at his prayers'.

Very distressing was the first occasion on which Storey encountered sudden death. Having lit two candles on a table in the bedroom of a small house, he was about to administer Communion to a sick parishioner, a big, heavy man with heart disease who had got out of bed to kneel down beside him; but who, dying instantly, suddenly fell on top of Storey, knocking him to the floor. There was no phone in the house, no-one else was there, and there was no-one next door, everyone being either out at work or otherwise in town. We do not know how he dealt with the situation, except that he remembered making 'a mess of all the arrangements', being 'very deeply' shaken. On another occasion, in answer to the question 'why do you think so highly about Fr. Storey?', a widow replied:

When my husband was dying I called him out at night. He came, greeted my husband and said some prayers. Then my husband asked Fr. Storey to help him up into a sitting position, which he did, holding him in that position with his arm round my husband's back. After a few moments my husband breathed his last. Fr. Storey laid him down. He said to me 'do you have anybody to wash the body?' I said 'No, Father'. He said 'bring me a bowl of warm water, soap and a towel', And there and then he washed my husband's body and laid him out.

The question had been put by Fr. Brian Passman, Storey's successor as curate at St. Joseph's.

Storey's evident commitment to Catholic Action was largely expressed at this stage through involvement with the Young Christian Worker movement and within a couple of years of his arrival St. Joseph's had sections for both men and women. It was possibly this which prompted Bishop Shine to give him a task beyond the parish. A Society of Catholic Students was formed, with the Bishop as Patron, two prominent lay people as President and Secretary respectively, and Storey as 'Ecclesiastical Assistant'. It aimed to provide 'a training ground for Catholics who will champion the Faith, more especially in the professional circles of Teesside'. Membership was open to men and women between the ages of 16 and 30 who were present or past students of universities, training colleges or the senior forms of schools. Its objectives were so reminiscent of Storey's work for the Higher Religious Certificate at Stonyhurst and his subsequent membership of the Catholic Evidence Guild that the Society may have been his suggestion. However, while substantial notices about it were published in the diocesan *Almanac & Directory* in both 1948 and 1949, it was not heard of again. As at Hull, such societies flourished *within* universities, especially after the expansion of higher education which followed the Robbins Report of 1963, but failed to get off the ground at a broader level in the diocese of Middlesbrough.

Regular contact with younger Catholics led Storey to join the diocesan group which participated in the national pilgrimage to the Lady shrine at Walsingham in July 1948. This was organised in response to Pope Pius XII's plea for penance and prayer in atonement for wartime evils. Fourteen groups set out for Walsingham from different locations, each carrying a huge oak cross weighing up to 100 lbs. At 236 miles the Middlesbrough leg was the longest and, with 25 men (including Storey) walking the entire way and several others joining them at various points, their group was one of the largest. Among them were Maurice Foley, the future senior Labour politician, then aged 22 and a member of the Young Christian Worker movement; 19-year-old Ambrose Griffiths, who joined the group at Pickering, and later succeeded Basil Hume as Abbot of Ampleforth, and later still became Bishop of Hexham and Newcastle; and Herbert McCabe, born and bred in Middlesbrough, then aged 21 and just graduated in Chemistry and Philosophy from the University of Manchester: during the pilgrimage he announced his intention of joining the Dominicans, which he did later that year. Storey and his brother, Peter, were two of the group's three chaplains.

A doctor organised training walks for several weeks previously, for which even the very fit Storey was subsequently grateful. Averaging over 20 and once walking 36 miles in a day, their route took them over the Cleveland Hills and the high moors to Egton Bridge. They then crossed the Vale of Pickering to Malton before going over the Wolds via Driffield. From there the going got gentler as they dropped down to Hull before crossing the Humber on the old paddle-steamer *Lincoln Castle* to New Holland and Grimsby. Then they went over the Lincolnshire Wolds to Louth and Spilsby before walking for long, flat days across the fens from Boston to King's Lynn. The wooded, undulating hills of Norfolk were a relief, though long before Walsingham, they were exhausted. The route was somewhat zig-zag because they had to identify overnight stopping places in advance, none of which offered more than a floor to lie on. The day ended with the service of Compline at 10 pm, with reveille each morning at 6.30 am for Mass and breakfast.

Each hour they made a station of the cross, but on three occasions the cross was blown down by strong winds. On the third occasion the main shaft split: a village smith-cum-joiner repaired it and made stronger supports which, however, added to its weight. The order of march was in threes, led by those carrying the cross, followed by a trio saying the rosary; these then took the cross, the next trio starting the rosary, and the front team returned to the rear. Those currently not involved walked behind them. One team, which included Herbert McCabe, soon became known as the 'heavies', turned to towards the end of a day or at other times when the going was tough. They took their midday break at a roadside inn, enduring 'the discipline of a spiritual or theological conference led by one of the chaplains, to the amusement of the publicans'. Storey remembered one at North Grimston on 'The Mystical Body' and another at the Saracen's Head Inn in the fenlands on 'The Nature of Grace'. Two 'outriders' distributed leaflets, telling people about the Pilgrimage as they passed. Each day one of them bicycled ahead to organise the night's accommodation.

At Walsingham rockets were sent up from each of the fourteen groups, who were joined by pilgrims who had travelled from their own area. After staying up all night at the shrine the Middlesbrough contingent celebrated with the others the first of fourteen consecutive Masses, with a fifteenth being added by a French contingent from Boulogne. Cardinal Griffin, head of the English Catholic Church, celebrated a Pontifical High Mass during which Storey fell 'asleep upright, held from falling simply by the crush of those in the close crowd'. After a break, some food and a 'fabulous paddle and foot-cooling' in the nearby River Stiffkey, each group carried its cross a further mile to the site of the ancient shrine.

Storey participated in some later Student Cross walks and in 1998 contributed to the fiftieth anniversary booklet of the original pilgrimage. For him, as for many of the others who took part, the walk in 1948 was a deeply significant episode: he had been brought up to have a special devotion to Our Lady and, as we have seen, was no stranger to Walsingham. The venture also anchored his growing personal commitment to the spiritual welfare of young people, especially those about to embark on their careers. It engendered lifelong friendships too, particularly with Fr. Herbert McCabe who, along with other Dominicans such as Fr. Lawrence Bright, was a regular visitor to the University of Hull while Storey was Chaplain there.

As a priest and counsellor Storey drew on vast pastoral experience and his early years as a curate in post-war Middlesbrough made a substantial, early contribution to this reservoir. Certain of his experiences were particularly influential in shaping his outlook and attitudes.

One of his duties at St. Joseph's was as Chaplain at St. Luke's, the Cleveland Mental Hospital, established in 1898. During his first year circumstances appeared to him to be completely unreformed since Victorian times, with burly male nurses manhandling patients, whose behaviour was often wild and uncontrolled – a true bedlam. Padded cells were used frequently and movement around the building was constantly constrained by locked and bolted doors. Psychiatry was then in its infancy: after the war there was also an acute shortage of trained personnel; the drugs which had been developed in wartime, and which were soon to be so helpful, were not yet in general circulation; and some of the treatments were primitive and wrong-headed. For example, because malaria and syphilis were thought to work against each other, many suffering from venereal disease (and there *were* many after the war) were deliberately infected with malaria and their temperatures kept at dangerously high levels, but with little or no effect.

He 'saw appalling things, but also very moving things'. One man, hearing a prayer from Storey, opened his eyes and said 'But I am Jesus', and died.

> Another who'd been very badly out of his mind and I was just giving him the last rites before he was dying, and he opened his eyes and said: 'Thank you, Father, for always treating me with respect: even though I was in a hopeless state, I always heard you. Thank you', and died. That taught me a supreme lesson....never to deal with the person who's got mental problems or mental deficiencies or learning difficulties as though they weren't absolutely whole. Even if they say they are Napoleon or Jesus Christ or whoever, treat it with respect.

He maintained that these incidents stood him in good stead later as a University Chaplain: in Hull 'there was a very schizophrenic case..[but]..I realised the importance of respect for the person'.

The significance of these lessons was driven home to him when the regime at St. Luke's changed dramatically. During the course of 1947, following the retirement of his predecessor, a Dr. T.M. Cuthbert was appointed Physician Superintendent. He immediately - 'almost overnight' – instituted wholesale changes. The bullying nurses were retired or removed, the padded cells disappeared, as did the reliance on lock-up, and a range of new medicines was introduced along with new treatments such as electro-convulsive therapy. Above all, Cuthbert gathered a highly competent team around him who, together, purveyed a new understanding of psychiatry. He also took care to explain to individual colleagues, even part-timers such as Storey, 'the new treatments and the new way of looking at things'.

> He was a great man and he taught me a great deal. I had some very deep relationships and friendships with the people in the hospital. I look back on that as the most fruitful time of my life, I think, in teaching *me* about humanity and about the problems we can have; but also teaching me how to respect, respect for the person, beginning to hammer it onto my mind in a way it hadn't [been] done at college or before.

Dr. Cuthbert stayed on at St. Luke's for the rest of his career, retiring in 1974, having served terms as President of the Royal Medico-Psychological Association, and of the Royal College of Psychiatrists. At St. Luke's Storey learned a great deal about a variety of mental conditions. In teaching him how best to approach each individual personality Cuthbert was a seminal influence, both on Storey himself and on the quality of his counselling.

The net result of another responsibility which came his way was less positive: in fact it was a valuable but largely negative experience. It took time to establish the social services recommended in the Beveridge Report and for several years church and other organisations tried, with varying success, to plug some of the gaps. The diocese of Middlesbrough established a Rescue Society in 1943. This was a Catholic effort to look after what contemporaries regarded as wayward girls and the children born to them out of wedlock, as well as to oversee the welfare of children who had been adopted or were fostered. The Society's Patron was Bishop Shine with Canon McMullan as President, but it was younger priests, initially Fr. Michael Lynam and then Fr. Chris Keating, who ran the show with the help of volunteers. They worked closely with the Sisters of Nazareth who managed two homes: St. Teresa's in Middlesbrough for recent mothers and their babies, and Nazareth House at Brough, near Hull in the south of the diocese, which took children up to two years old.

Although he had some involvement with the Society's work from 1947, Storey was appointed Assistant Administrator of it in 1951 and Administrator a year later.

> I found myself going round the diocese on a James motorbike and rescuing anyone appealing for help – an unmarried girl or parents wanting a child adopted or whatever it might be….And it was a moving time, although absolutely without training for me.

He vividly recalled one episode. He had persuaded another priest to join him in conveying an infant over the 84 miles from St. Teresa's in Middlesbrough to Nazareth House in Brough, 'with the baby wrapped up by the nuns'. Outside York their car was halted behind a serious road accident, so there was delay and much police activity. One constable, suddenly spotting an unattended baby in the back of a vehicle, with two gentlemen in full clerical fig, as they were, in the front, became extremely interrogative – but eventually let them on their way.

> That was the way of it then, often picking up children in funny places or trying to rescue girls and get them into homes….There was very little care of girls having babies taken off them even though they didn't wish it at all. I remember one girl didn't even see her child. She was told it would be better if the baby's adoptive parents were there straight away and the child was taken away….I've known her since – she's been in and out of mental hospitals all her life….Somehow one thought it was for their welfare.

He particularly remembered a young man from his parish who was on remand for murder. Having discovered that he had been adopted and that his parents were not his real parents, he had shot them both. 'That triggered the determination that adopted children should always be told they were adopted'. And as for the girls, 'such lovely girls and often so distressed and so disgraced ....one wonders how they survived afterwards'. It was 'quite a time and I'm glad I eventually left that and was moved out' to different work. He was, however, responsible for one significant change. Initially and for several years, advertisements relating to the Rescue Society stated, in regard to babies, that 'first cases only' were accepted: that statement disappeared during Storey's time and did not return.

Like any other priest, Storey's key role in the midst of these various challenges was at the altar: there was little point in good works if what happened in church was less than appropriate. While instinctively supportive of the notion of Catholic Action by the laity, he was also discomfited by the contrast between this and the exceedingly passive role allowed to them in church. This was why he had warmly welcomed the stress on the significance of their role in the encyclical *Mystici Corporis* in 1943. There was further good news on this front in November 1947 when Pius XII issued the encyclical *Mediator Dei.* Liturgy, it argued, was not merely a series of impressive and colourful ceremonies: it was the Church at worship. The encyclical explicitly advocated the active participation of the laity in the liturgy and, indeed, in parish life as a whole. In particular, 'the Mass was the people's sacrifice as well as the priest's, and everybody should take part in it'.

People forget, you know, that up to that time you didn't say 'Amen', even if you were in the congregation during the Mass - only the altar boys did that. This was all in Latin: you took no part in it whatever. And suddenly it was what you call dialogue where you'd be saying some of the words together.

Also, because the Eucharist was a renewal of Christ's sacrifice on the cross, the faithful were encouraged to take communion regularly.

> And the bread should be real bread, if possible, and it should be broken. And the beginning of the notion that you should be drinking from the chalice, and that the laity should have participation in this. This was an extraordinary beginning of a move in a different direction, of opening up.

The thrust of the encyclical influenced the direction of further reforms during Vatican II and Storey welcomed it warmly. It was 'dynamite to me' and the bedrock of what he came to describe towards the end of his life as 'collaborative ministry'.

For many years after his death in 1958 Pius XII's career, both before and after he became Pope, particularly while in Germany and especially *vis-a-vis* the Holocaust, was a matter of fierce controversy; and this continues to be the case, with many still arguing that for the sake of German Catholicism the Pope made too many compromises with Hitler's regime and, in particular, failed to support Jews as strongly as he should have done. Storey passed no judgement on these issues, but always maintained that the controversy overshadowed and obscured the value of these two encyclicals of the 1940s, which he regarded as 'seed documents of what was going to happen later' in Vatican II. In noting his view we should bear in mind that he was no slavish devotee of the papacy. In 1950, for example, each Catholic parish was asked to sign a petition asking the Pope to define the Assumption of Mary as a dogma and, therefore, part of the faith. While Storey had no difficulty with what he described as 'a very lovely doctrine', he felt that it 'wasn't capable of definition'; and much to the annoyance of Canon McMullan, refused to sign. More generally, he continued to feel that papal infallibility:

> has been terribly overstated. It's only been used twice in all

history, once was the Immaculate Conception and the other was the Feast of the Assumption; and on both occasions it was with the consent of the whole Church and with the wishes of the whole Church.

He felt that the overstatement did 'a lot of damage to people because they think everything the Pope says has to carry with it this mark of infallibility, which of course it does not'.

During these busy post-war years Storey was deeply affected by two personal developments. One of them was closely connected with his other work at St. Joseph's. In addition to the church, the presbytery and the men's club, there was a primary school on the site with a staff of about ten, with two nuns in charge, two male teachers and the remainder female. Both curates came into school at the beginning of each day and gave religious instruction for the first half hour: dividing the school between them, they each taught one group one morning, and the other on the following day, and so on in turn.

I enjoyed that very much although I wasn't as good as the teachers, I am sure, at dealing with five-year-olds and seven-year-olds and so on; but it was a wonderful experience and I loved the teaching in the school and the great work with that community….It was an exhilarating time.

They gradually got to know all the pupils and from an earlier stage knew the teachers very well.

Like Storey, one of the staff, a young woman, had just finished her training and embarked on her career. She came from the rural area to the south, near Whitby. She 'hadn't had, I think, any relationships with anyone. She was a lovely person'. Her name was Mildred Mary Raw, always referred to by Storey simply as M. The two of them fell 'absolutely head over heels in love, madly in love'.

It was really quite explosive; for the first ever time I had actually fallen in love with somebody….We had to keep it pretty secret but for many years it was a great personal relationship we had….She wasn't wanting to marry and I wasn't in a position to be able to do so. And yet on the other hand we were absolutely at one; and a great blessing to me was I didn't need to go for freedom.

Their relationship was celibate throughout, as he was careful to confirm, but none the less ardent for that. It caused them great stress but also brought deep joy, constituting the foreground to everything that happened to them over many years. It continued for over two decades and we will return to it in more detail later.

The other personal matter was the death of Storey's father, George Snowden Storey. His relations with his parents were clearly influenced by the fact that they were a large family: with a taxing job his father could not develop a similarly close relationship with the six children born between 1911 and 1919.

My experience with my own family was love. My Mum and Dad had a great love for one another and a great love for us; but I was number six and [we] had come in fairly quick succession and I suppose being number six I didn't feel a very great closeness to my Dad. He was always out at work and looking after the elder brothers, and my Mum, I think, was close to me.

He then had, with only short breaks, years away at school, seminary and university. His father moved posts from Warter back to Everingham in 1938 but 'the management of the Everingham estate became increasingly onerous'. George was clearly failing by the early 1940s. Once he was evacuated from Italy Storey saw something of him during vacations. After his ordination he came back to Everingham to celebrate his second Mass. By then George was ill, with what we do not know, and the tragic death of Gerard Storey a month later 'was, as it were, the last straw'.

> He retired to an old rectory at Harswell: and though physically…. strong - he was still hunting this last Christmas [1946] at the age of 71 - he was mentally tired. The end came rather quickly and most holily on May 4th [1947], his son, Fr. Anthony Storey being with him till the last.

Storey got to know his father really well, therefore, only in George's last years. He not only regretted this. The circumstances which brought it about had a strong influence on his attitude towards marriage and family matters - particularly the ethics of contraception - for the rest of his life.

By the early 1950s, with Bishop Shine ailing, the diocese was being run by his Auxiliary, Bishop George Brunner. Consecrated in 1946, he had originally been based in the south of the diocese at Hull but by now had moved north to Bishop's House in Middlesbrough. In 1952 he decided to move Storey from St. Joseph's to the nearby parish of Corpus Christi.

From 1936 services there had been held in a small Mass Centre and conducted by priests from North Ormesby. However, the Centre was completely destroyed by fire in 1943 and, when suitable alternative premises could not be found, it was decided to build. Amidst wartime shortages and post-war red tape, this was easier said than done. Work eventually began in 1948, entirely by voluntary labour except for a single paid overseer, and with most of the materials being second-hand. The building, housing both a church and (prior to the building of a new school) temporary classrooms, was opened in May 1949. By the time Storey became Curate to the Parish Priest, Fr. Michael Lynam, in 1952 a presbytery had also been completed.

The parish served the Brambles Farm and Thorntree estates

which had some 2,000 Catholics. Development there had come rather later than at Grove Hill, but its central purpose - the expansion of Middlesbrough's stock of public housing - was identical. So there was little if any change in the nature of Storey's duties. His arrival came at the time of his heaviest involvement with the Diocesan Rescue Service. It seems that his move was motivated primarily by the wish to get the school off to a good start in its new premises, which were completed at a cost of almost £100,000 and opened in October 1954. There were features of the work of the Rescue Society which left Storey feeling distinctly uneasy; and when, after less than two years and 'at very short notice', Bishop Brunner asked him to move on again, he was relieved to do so.

His new responsibilities were located not far from Middlesbrough, in the parish of Our Lady of Lourdes on the north-east coast at Saltburn-by-the-Sea; but the parishes were very different. The Parish Priest was Canon John Chadwick from Drogheda who had been trained at Ushaw for the Middlesbrough diocese; and who, apart from a one-year stint as Bishop's Secretary, had served continuously at St. Wilfrid's parish in York before coming to Saltburn in 1943. According to Storey, Chadwick 'was an old-style clergyman' who 'had a strict exterior and rigidly defended the Church law and [its] rules; [but] inwardly [he was] the kindest man'. He had celebrated the golden jubilee of his ordination in 1954 while in a Whitby nursing home. He wished to return to Saltburn but, largely bedridden and now dying, was incapable of running the parish. Storey was asked to do so and also to look after the Canon: it 'was my first real entry into the nursing world of the dying and the really distressed'.

Although there were only about 390 Catholics in the parish (including some 40 Poles), there was plenty for one priest to do. There was a chapel of ease, St. Bede's, at Marske-by-the-Sea, and three Masses were said each Sunday, one there and two in

Saltburn. There was also a maternity home at Overdene and an Old Folks' home to keep an eye on. Following the earlier sale of a hall, parish debts were low, so there was no financial anxiety and the wolf was kept from the door by a medley of church collections, a church door box, raffles, whist drives and sales of work. Fr. Chadwick had visited parishioners very regularly but had sometimes been refused access to a house 'where he'd threatened Hell if they didn't go to Mass'. Then he would worry that he might be damned for being rude by waving his stick. Storey 'came to love him, as did his parishioners'. On Mondays, if well enough, the Canon called a taxi to take them both to the Alexandra Hotel for lunch, carrying a bottle of wine in his morning coat. On arrival he placed the bottle firmly in the middle of their table and the waiter invariably raised no objection.

It was as well that the presbytery could comfortably accommodate both of them because before long Canon Chadwick became extremely ill and had to be looked after night and day. He was very fastidious and refused to allow any nurse or woman to touch him; this was perhaps why he had left the nursing home and returned to the presbytery in Saltburn. Consequently, with a great deal of help from a caring doctor, Richard Macauliffe, Storey had to do virtually everything for him, 'clean him up and change sheets and all those kinds of things' as he became incontinent. As the Canon once said 'with a twinkle in his eye', 'it happens, you know, even in the best of families'. Storey also read the bible to him.

> He told me which book he wanted to read and I would read for hours. It's surprising how long he could attend before falling off to sleep, and then sometimes he'd stop me and get me to re-read a passage, or he'd make some wry comment about the different passages and the different incidents. My hunger for the bible really was increased enormously. His great enthusiasm to hear the word of God

deeply affected me during the rest of the time I spent with him.

While others covered for him, Storey was sometimes able to get a break. He played cricket locally and went swimming at Saltburn Nab – 'it took all summer for the sea to get warm'. He also looked at the wildlife and became 'deeply interested in marine life'. He walked on the moors, examining rocks and stones, and once saw 'an adder going right past me on the bank looking so beautiful'. In the presbytery, on the Canon's better days, they spent a lot of time talking about European history, which they both loved; and no doubt Storey explored the Canon's library, which contained many books about the Venerable Bede and his contemporaries.

'But it was a stressful time'. In addition to his other ailments Fr. Chadwick suffered from obsessive compulsive disorder, a condition Storey was familiar with from his time at St. Luke's. Had he locked the church door? He, not Storey, must go and check. So he would check, find that he had already done so, and then return to the original question some time later; and the same action would follow. The problem extended to parishioners.

Have I spoken roughly to that person? Perhaps I'll be punished for it. I'd better go back and speak more kindly to them. Oh dear, perhaps I ought to have spoken more sternly to them because they aren't behaving right; will I be punished for that?

He had been fond of his former housekeeper, who had served him in York and Saltburn for many years and been buried in the cemetery at Saltburn. As his own death approached he wondered whether he might be buried next to her. But would that give scandal to people and, if so, perhaps he should be buried in another cemetery? Fortunately for the Canon and for Storey, he became very calm and peaceful towards the end. He died in his presbytery on 23 May 1955 and was buried next to his housekeeper. So, while 'it was a very happy ending….it had been a sad time'.

The sequel was that Storey himself 'had a very bad nervous breakdown'. He passed no comment on the reason why this occurred, other than that he had found looking after Canon Chadwick very stressful. Some strain also derived from his relationship with Mildred; and for eight years his other duties, while in many respects satisfying, had stretched him. So his breakdown was perhaps due to a combination of factors. We do not know. Nor, perhaps, did he. Bishop Brunner told him to take three months off to restore himself. Characteristically, he decided to take a long, solitary walk through northern Italy.

Carrying a single rucksack, he travelled by rail to Florence and then by bus to Arezzo, some 50 miles to the south-east, where he saw the glorious frescoes of Piero della Francesca for the first time. From there he walked westwards through Cortona and across the Tuscan hills, and then on to Lake Trasimene and Perugia in Umbria. One night he stayed with an elderly parish priest who, having little money, found paid work in the tobacco fields. Next morning they said Mass together:

> one after the other because we weren't concelebrating in those days. And then he led me up on to the tops above Lake Trasimene, where we stood at the source of a stream; and he told me the stream was called the 'Sanguinetto', which was the stream where Hannibal had routed the Romans and the stream ran with blood. And about a thousand [*sic*] years later it's still called the 'Sanguinetto'. And while we were there the first spring swallow came up the valley and over our heads; and he bade me adieu.

Turning south-eastwards again, Storey walked on, down the

railway line and across the River Tiber to Assisi. On foot it was a very long journey indeed: 'a strange experience, being absolutely alone in a country [and] not knowing where you're going to stay the next night'.

Although walking, preferably on high ground, was among his favourite pastimes, there were particular reasons why he chose to do so in Italy. He had taken Francis as his Confirmation name and had read a great deal about St. Francis and his colleagues. 'I'd always wanted to become a Franciscan in my earlier years and had a great longing to go and visit [Assisi] on pilgrimage'. On this, his first visit, he approached the hill town at sunset and 'it was looking gorgeous'. However, some great white sheepdogs came bounding towards him across a field and, briefly, he thought he was in trouble until the farmer quietened them. He gave Storey some sausage and wine.

> He was telling me with tears in his eyes that his son had just become a brother Franciscan in the monastery there and he was going to make his vows at Easter; and he cried at the wonder of it. And then I went up to the tomb of St. Francis. It was a great day for me, like becoming a completely new person. By then I'd had six days all by myself, wandering around Assisi where there were no visitors at all.

The unusual remedy that he had prescribed for himself had worked wonderfully well: he felt whole again.

CHAPTER SIX

HULL 1955-62

As soon as Storey returned from Italy Bishop Brunner sent him as Curate to the parish of St. Charles Borromeo in the centre of Hull, where Fr. Paddy McEnroe had preceded him. In contrast to Middlesbrough, which had grown from the mid-19th century, the city had a long history. It was the major port on the east coast, nationally third in importance to London and Liverpool. With just under 300,000 inhabitants it was much larger than Middlesbrough and in fishing had an old-established industry. It had suffered much more extensive war damage than Teesside. The city lay next to the River Hull and the coast, so it had been easy for German bombers to find it. There were raids throughout the war, but the worst were in 1941. Civilian casualties were relatively light because up to a third of the population temporarily exited the city for the countryside during the worst of the bombing. Somehow, 'among the ruins all around', the church of St. Charles in Jarratt St. emerged unscathed, but much of the rest of the city centre was devastated. 'Over 5,000 houses were destroyed, with half the central shopping area; three million square feet of factory space, including two of the three flour mills and several oil and cake mills; [and] 27 churches and 14 school and hospital buildings'. The damage was akin to that suffered by Plymouth and the total cost (at 1952 prices) possibly exceeded £20M. A plan for reconstruction was accepted as early as 1945 and Storey witnessed much of its implementation during the later 1950s.

Along with the Cathedral community in Middlesbrough and

St. Wilfrid's in York, the parish of St. Charles in Hull was a major diocesan focal point and one with which Bishop Brunner had long been associated. His family, watchmakers and jewellers of German extraction, had lived in Hull for over 150 years before his birth in 1889. For over three decades following ordination in 1917 he worked either in Hull or nearby, firstly at St. Charles, briefly at Hessle, then as parish priest at St. Patrick's in the city, and from 1937 as parish priest of St. Charles. He was appointed Auxiliary Bishop in 1946, but stayed in Hull until 1951 when he moved to Middlesbrough as Vicar General. There he gradually took over from the ailing Bishop Shine; got to know of Storey's work on the new estates; singled him out to deal with the crisis in Saltburn; and after his breakdown allowed him to find his own route to recovery. He must have been impressed by Storey's record and abilities, as he was by Paddy McEnroe, Storey's predecessor as curate, who now took up a post with the B.B.C. Bishop Brunner also asked Storey to do some teaching of history and religion on a part-time basis at St. Mary's School in the city. No-one knew better than the bishop the size of the task at St. Charles: 'the building into life of a parish that was dying from the weariness and ravages of war'.

The bishop also knew from personal experience that his successor at St. Charles, Fr. James Knowles, was a leader of character and ability. An ex-army chaplain mentioned in despatches, he had been involved in the evacuation from Dunkirk, later served in North Africa, Sicily and Greece, and was present at the liberation of Rome. Appointed Curate at St. Charles after the war, he became Parish Priest in 1951 when Bishop Brunner moved to Middlesbrough. He proved a hard taskmaster, generating a whirlwind of activity and expecting wholehearted commitment from his curates: in return they could anticipate firm judgement, clear guidance and total loyalty. Besides Storey, there was another curate, Fr. Kevin Coughlan, ten years his junior; and the Port Chaplain, Fr. Maurice Hardy, also lived in the presbytery.

Storey replaced Paddy McEnroe, who succeeded Fr. Agnellus Andrew at the B.B.C. in Manchester when the latter was promoted to London (and ultimately replaced him there when Fr. Andrew retired in 1967). For some time after his appointment, however, Fr. McEnroe retained a base in the presbytery in Hull. Earlier he had given Fr. Knowles a very good press; and when Storey brashly enquired whether his new parish priest would need pushing along, had laughed and said: 'He'll push you, boy, but he needs holding or he'll burn himself out'. Sadly, this proved prophetic because Fr. Knowles died suddenly in 1964, aged only 53. So Storey 'much looked forward' to his new post. According to Fr. Charles Heslin, formerly at St. Charles and latterly Storey's neighbour in Saltburn, it was 'just the appointment for you, Tony'.

If Storey felt he had been sufficiently hardened by his experiences in Middlesbrough, he was wrong. He was deeply shocked and depressed by the conditions he encountered in Hull. There had been a good deal of slum clearance in the west of the city, but much remained to be done elsewhere.

> All sorts of things I couldn't understand at all, great poverty of the little side streets where there would be just one tap for the whole terrace and still the soil clearance carts, the little buckets to be cleared away. And nobody could have a bath, [though] there were public baths; after all there was no water in the house[s] or anything like that.

Liaising with doctors and welfare officers, Storey toured the slums on bicycle, getting to know his new parishioners and, where he could, trying to help them cope with the worst effects 'of poverty [which] was quite surprising, quite shocking'.

Houses were infested very badly. The wallpaper had been

put on again and again, so there were a lot of bugs behind the wallpaper. Sometimes the wallpaper could be 10 or 15 layers thick because they'd put a new one up….with flour and paste and the bugs would be living on that. And the pest control man would come in and he'd smell what was the trouble and oh dear there were no proper sheets and bed bugs and so on. I found people when they were dying and you were doing the last rites, you would find there were lice all over the place in the bed and bed bugs too.

Compared with Middlesbrough or Saltburn, it was 'very distressing'.

As he began to come to terms with his new situation Storey was extremely busy. Fr. Knowles divided the parish into three precincts and he and his two curates looked after one each: he took the north end, Fr. Coughlan had the old town to the east, and Storey the area in between. Families were visited systematically, and any services (baptisms, funerals, etc.) required by parishioners were conducted by the priest responsible for their area. Kingston General Hospital was visited daily, as were St. Charles Boys' School in Pryme St. and St. Gregory's Girls' School in Scott St. There were sessions for couples planning to marry and for would-be converts. Each of the parish's wide variety of organisations looked for some support from a priest: the St. Vincent de Paul Society, the Union of Catholic Mothers, the Confraternity of the Blessed Sacrament, the Legion of Mary, the Knights of St. Columba and the Catholic Social Guild. The parish was large and it was common during the 1950s for the three Sunday morning Masses to attract a total congregation of 1,200 people. There were other services both on Sundays and weekdays, and the confessionals were manned every day of the week except Sunday. His job was very large in relation to earlier ones, which was perhaps what Fr. Heslin had in mind when commenting on Storey's appointment.

As at St. Joseph's in Grove Hill, the two curates divided the Youth Clubs between them, Kevin Coughlan supervising the girls and Storey the boys, although all the priests resident in the parish and many of their friends were drawn in to help. With an entrance fee of three old pence, the Boys' Club started in the Rectory cellar soon after Storey's arrival. Besides billiards, darts and judo, the main sports were boxing and rugby, and his chief responsibility, requiring a change of code from Union, was to manage the Rugby League teams. On one occasion, having started a mass brawl in the middle of a match, St. Charles's entire Under-18 side was sent off. Storey was summoned 'before the beaks' at Craven Park, the local League headquarters, and made sure that he was wearing his collar and looking 'very clerical'.

> They didn't quite know what to do with this priest who was running this wild youth club with wicked people. They were pretty wicked boys, I must say; and when I was in a scrum with them or in any kind of tackle you weren't sure what part of you was going to be damaged - they were rough, rough lads.

Storey thought it a 'great experience' and loved his time with them. Both clubs prospered and in October 1960 a new Youth Centre was opened in Lockwood St.

For much of the period before Storey arrived Fr. Knowles was pre-occupied with restoring his church to its former glory. According to Pevsner, its 'restrained exterior', flush with adjacent buildings and not even looking like a church, 'does not prepare one for the striking baroque interior'. In the view of another commentator, re-modelling during the 19th century had created 'one of the most opulent and dramatic interiors of any… .church in England - a fantastical Roman church with a heavy touch of Austrian rococo'. Though not fundamental, wartime damage had left it in 'a dreadful state' and the decoration of the entire building, and much else, needed careful and costly attention. Characteristically acting as his own project manager, Fr. Knowles completed this, in three phases, by the mid-1950s.

He insisted on impeccable presentation of the liturgy, which Storey hugely appreciated.

> Behind all this was a mind correctly centred – the church, the beauty of God's House came first; the ceremonies must be done well, the times made suitable, the sacraments made daily available. He took the greatest care about these things, and was touchy to a degree about the slipshod.

While this re-inforced Storey's own instincts, he was initially hesitant but ultimately learned a good deal from another feature of Knowles's management.

> He would put on services to suit the variant tastes or capacities of the very different levels of his people; some of these seemed maudlin, some sheer stunts, some sheer genius - but he was right. He knew full well the very marked divergence between what helps the devotion of one area of his people from what helps others. His taste in planning services was catholic, and bore immense fruit.

The parish was run like a military operation, and there was no doubt as to who was the commanding officer. After Kevin Coughlan had discharged one arduous task splendidly, he was told: 'we expect this at St. Charles'. And one Sunday, when Storey apologised at supper for a poor performance, having lost his thread during a sermon, his boss reminded him that 'I decide whether there is a bad performance or not in this church, Father'. Knowles soon concluded that Storey's preaching was 'sound and colourful'. Storey regarded Knowles's sermons - always written out in full but nonchalantly delivered - as 'very often sheer gold'. What he particularly valued in Fr. Knowles was his constant availability: the door of his office was left ajar, so there was regular engagement with his curates and many others. Although Storey confessed to 'moments of jealous anger at the way the old and sick and poor would always in their need ask for and long only to see' Fr. Knowles, he deeply respected his 'unerring courtesy and readiness to give attention to any and every person who came to him', a trait which he himself sought to emulate. In an unwitting reflection of what many came later to feel about Storey himself, he also said: 'whenever I had any personal problem, there was no man I would rather go to for the clear unravelling of my mixed-up soul'.

The art of leadership, however, involves not just clarity of purpose, a broad perspective on the way ahead, and openness to both clients and colleagues, but also the ability to recognise gifts in subordinates that one does not possess or is unable at times to exercise oneself; and in Storey's case this was where Knowles excelled. He strongly encouraged him to display his talents as a communicator about the faith.

> There was a great surge of people wanting to receive instruction about what was the nature of the Church. Both the Catholic Church and [the] Quakers started advertising talks on the faith and there was a very big response.

Although Fr. Knowles supported him, it appears that the initiative for this came originally from Storey. His three months' leave following Canon Chadwick's death on 23 May 1955 implies that he arrived in Hull in late August or early September. Yet, seemingly at his own suggestion, he embarked on 20 September on a series of 12 talks for non-Catholics, widely publicised, including on a banner hung from the church facade. They were delivered in St. Charles's Social Centre and proved very popular, with never fewer than 80 present at individual sessions and 50 of them attending all of them. He repeated this series during the following autumn, when it ran alongside a series of talks for

Catholics with which he sometimes received help from other priests. A new eight-week series for non-Catholics began in February 1957. And then, starting on 24 September 1958 and under the auspices of the Hull Branch of the Workers' Educational Association, Storey delivered a 24-week course on 'The Personality and Work of Jesus Christ'. Since the previous May he had been in touch with the District Secretary of the Hull branch who, though keen to emphasise that his organisation could not be 'associated with any particular views on the subject', was very supportive, as was Hull's Chief Librarian, who reserved items from the booklist. The course was delivered on Wednesdays in St. Charles's Boys' School and, as a gesture of goodwill from Fr. Knowles, the parish offered the school to the W.E.A. 'for up to three other classes on any subjects if required'. A further series of talks for non-Catholics was delivered in May, June and July 1960.

These and analogous activities were a highlight of his period at St. Charles and Storey stated clearly why he felt they were so important.

> Never has it been more necessary for the ordinary Catholic - not merely for the specialist, the priest or teacher, but for the ordinary man or woman – to have the content of the Faith clearly in his mind. He must know it in terms that he himself can understand and that he can turn easily into words, so as to explain and defend these great truths in the widening field of day-to-day exchange.

These views originated in his decision to take and repeat the Higher Religious Certificate at Stonyhurst and then to join the Catholic Evidence Guild. In his view the laity were deprived of their rightful place in the liturgy and in everything else to do with the life of the Church. Nevertheless, partly as a consequence of this and with few exceptions, they themselves had too flimsy a grasp of the detail of what they claimed to believe, and were correspondingly ill-equipped to defend or promote it. A leading aim of his priestly life, wherever he went, was to remedy this.

There were other ways in which he exercised his gift for talking or writing about matters of faith lucidly and persuasively. Among the innumerable calls on his time, Fr. Knowles edited the *Hull Catholic Magazine,* a publication which under him normally appeared six times a year. Produced for all parishes in the Hull area, it was substantial in format and content and contained news of parish arrangements, events and activities; articles and correspondence; a question box; and reviews. The question box feature dealt with a single query per issue and between those for Sept./Oct. 1956 and Aug./Sept. 1961 Storey contributed fourteen essays on topics such as 'Original Sin', 'Baptism', 'Cremation', 'Sex and Marriage', 'The World Council of Churches' and also, somewhat bizarrely, 'How can Our Lord be lonely in the tabernacle if he is also in heaven?' Knowles also regularly commissioned Storey as a reviewer, sometimes of as many as five, six or seven books in a single issue. While Werner Keller's *The Bible as History* 'can be recommended without reserve', a trio on family matters (one for boys, one for girls, and a third for mothers) was judged no more than 'sound'. He didn't pull punches: he grumbled about prices, while Hertha Pauli's *Christmas and the Saints* 'is frankly childish, and….too full of real error to be allowed to pass, even for small children'. One of his last contributions to the *Magazine* was 'Hull City Centre, 1961, After Anglia Tours Ltd.'. Wartime damage having finally been removed to make way for fresh development, this was a jocular survey of the new architecture beginning to grace the city.

In Hull, therefore, Storey built a reputation as an excellent communicator – someone who could write or talk about complex matters fluently and attractively. This led to other things. In 1956 he published an essay in the diocesan *Directory* on 'Our Lady's

Chapel at Mount Grace' near Osmotherley in north Yorkshire, an historic site above the remains of a dissolved Carthusian Priory which captivated both him and his brother, Peter. He developed an illustrated talk on 'The Holy Shroud' which he was often asked to repeat. In 1958 Bishop Brunner appointed him Ecclesiastical Assistant to the Hull Newman Circle. And on Sunday 29 January 1961 Fr. Knowles delegated to him the responsibility for preaching when 'The People's Service' was broadcast live on the B.B.C. from St. Charles. Shortly afterwards, amidst the promulgation of the cause for canonisation of the 40 English Martyrs, he wrote a piece for the *Directory* on 'What is a Martyr?' By the early 1960s he enjoyed a reputation as an outstanding priest, approachable, articulate and humane, and a gifted speaker and writer.

By the time of his appointment to St. Charles, and no doubt before then, Storey's qualities were keenly appreciated by those closest to him. According to his mother, writing to him in the mid-1950s, 'God has given you a gift of understanding and compassion for other people's troubles, for which I am most grateful'. However, very little family correspondence has survived for any period, though there are several letters to him from Agatha dating from 1956-57. These reveal a very open relationship between them in which they regularly discussed the problems encountered by Agatha and her acquaintances and which help to explain Storey's informed and sensitive counselling of couples in a way that was quite exceptional among Catholic priests of his generation.

In 1951, four years after George Storey's death, Harriet had moved to Bishop's Stortford in Hertfordshire to live with Agatha and her family, who were not that far from Patience in central London where Harriet had been educated. In 1944 at the age of 30 Agatha had married William Knapton, an army officer, and

21: Hull: Storey as Curate at St. Charles.

by 1956 they had two sons, Peter and Michael. The previous decade or so had been one of change for all of them. Harriet had successfully undergone some form of operation and was now living independently and apparently in reasonably good health for someone approaching 70. In 1949, suffering since a pre-war spell in Hong Kong from recurrent malaria and having reached the rank of Major-General, William left the army for a senior post in the civil service. In 1955 he was obliged on medical grounds to give up full-time work, though he continued to supplement his pension by serving on Civil Service Boards. Agatha had had a busy war, rising rapidly to a rank equivalent to a Lieutenant Colonel in the Auxiliary Territorial Service, the women's branch of the British Army. However, she had not enjoyed particularly good health since her marriage and by the mid-1950s was still striving for full fitness. She and William had moved from the house they had shared with Harriet and were now living at The

Grange, Greenstead Green, Essex.

In October 1956 Storey received a letter from Harriet telling him of a serious row between herself and Agatha: they had both said how difficult they found it to get on with each other, and Agatha had later confirmed this by letter. Harriet told her younger son because she knew how close Storey was to his older sister, and feared that his attitude towards her would be adversely affected by what Agatha might say. Storey immediately reassured his mother and then wrote to Agatha.

She could never have married, she said, for reasons other than love. She had consciously chosen 'worthwhile' work – as a hospital almoner – as an insurance against not finding the right partner. Having turned down several offers, she had married relatively late, but in William she had found her man. There was never any doubt about that on either side. Nevertheless, there were major difficulties with William's mother who, living well beyond her means, had been subsidised and regularly bailed out by William. Matters had improved only a year or so previously after Agatha had blown her top spectacularly with the 85-year-old Mrs. Knapton and her daughter. 'It did no end of good'. Only then had she been able to concentrate on her more immediate situation: not just her husband and children but her friends, some of whom had various moral, theological and relational problems on which they needed advice. A number of them also struggled either with the need to avoid pregnancy or a wish to achieve it.

Storey immediately became heavily involved in trying to help them. Significantly, it was during this period that he encountered Erich Fromm's *The Art of Loving*. The book was published in 1956 and recommended to him by a probation officer. Fromm argued that, while education in the modern world had become ever more varied, there was one yawning gap: there was virtually no systematic teaching or guidance in the art of loving and, therefore, little or no learning. Yet, though of primary importance to human happiness, between individuals, among families, and beyond, love was not magical or mysterious, something that could not be analysed or explained. Rather, it was a skill that could, and should, be taught, nurtured and developed. From this point onwards, recognising this as a fundamental and revolutionary truth, Storey espoused this personally and incorporated it in his approach to guidance and counselling.

At first the tone and content of Agatha's letters were full of anxiety. His response was to encourage her to write frequently and at length in the hope that articulating difficulties would help her and her friends to solve them. His replies were substantial and at one point, being very busy, she asked him not to write letters which demanded long replies for at least a month. He recommended books, sourcing and sending many of them, and consulted extensively among his acquaintances in the medical and paramedical professions. In January 1956 he had suggested that Agatha and her family join him for a trip to Italy, especially Assisi, in the following summer, but they could not afford to do so and, without him, visited a friend near Dublin instead. During the course of the year, however, matters steadily improved. She and Storey had frequent and extensive exchanges on a whole gamut of issues, not least sex, marriage and Catholicism.

She lamented people's lack of knowledge of sexual matters, citing herself as an example. 'I was so ignorant I did not know there was anything to learn. I thought it just happened and I'm sure there are lots like me'. Without personal experience or the opportunity or time to read everything he himself recommended, Storey occasionally came a cropper. Some of the doctors he talked to about the 'safe period' suggested that couples might be advised to proceed so far with love-making but stop short of intercourse. Agatha came down on this like a ton of bricks.

How can a couple make love to just such a point & then lay off before it gets out of control. I'd have thought it was asking for trouble....one would do better with *nothing* than the strain of keeping things short of the S[ex] A[ct]; it strikes me as an altogether unnatural suggestion....'Necking' in lieu of proper marital union. So there you are dear!

Agatha was also fiercely scornful of one set of 'horrible books' of moral theology, in which she:

hit upon passages dissecting the marriage act into 'sinless', 'sinful', 'partially sinful', etc. etc. in other words trying to undermine one's joy in the whole thing by making one conscious of 'motives', 'degrees' etc. etc. & introducing scruples.

Without an ounce of conviction, she said she 'would read them shortly'.

Ultimately, she and her friends singled out for special praise Baron Frederick von Gagern's *Difficulties in Married Life,* which 'they can hardly be without'. She also praised *The Marriage Manual*, written by an American non-Catholic couple, which provided illustrations of sexual activity. Particularly during the latter half of 1956, matters slowly but steadily prospered. Agatha's health was restored and before long William's doctors identified drugs which resolved his medical problems.

Agatha had regretted not having had a daughter and they now tried to remedy this. Ultimately, she came to accept that this was not to be. Nevertheless, with unremitting help from her priest brother, she reached a level of peace and contentment that she had not known previously. Storey must have been delighted for her (and for those of her friends he had advised) and gratified by the role he had been able to play: his contribution as a brother was noble; as a celibate priest it was remarkable.

Yet a triumph for them amounted to something very different for him. During the course of their long correspondence Agatha reverted to discussing her poor relationship with her mother; and she told Storey candidly what she felt had caused it. Following his birth, their parents had slept in separate rooms, with Agatha sharing with Harriet – this was why she could never understand or get on with her mother.

> The lack of a normal sex life in our parents (after you were born) was the beginning and end of all the tensions which were such a nightmare to me, I am *absolutely certain*. Mummy was in her 30s & Daddy in his 40s & they had separate bedrooms etc. for *good,* since they knew no other way out of the difficulty of endless pregnancies. Patience was the result of one single episode years later. If they had had the safe period & a normal periodic sex life, there never would have been the 'two camps' that I remember so well. Daddy v. Mother. I have never been able to be normal with either of them; it affected me much more than they had any idea. Mother declares that she never 'understood' me, but maybe we can improve that gradually now, I don't know.

In another letter she maintained that 'as for our poor parents, I think they had a ghastly time; they completely lost touch'. Immediately above this statement, in pencil, Storey wrote: 'I was too young to know this at all'.

Later he reported the change in the nature of his parents' marital arrangements as follows:

> We were all palmed off into separate bedrooms, some of the boy children with Daddy and Agatha with Mum. And they very rarely slept together and this was because they loved each other but were not allowed to practise any form of contraception.

This was a scaled-down version of Agatha's candid description of the situation and its lingering effects, which must have made very painful reading for him. We do not know for certain that it was from Agatha and at this stage that Storey *first* learned of the connection between his birth and the change in his parents' relations, but it appears likely that it was. There is no doubt, however, that this entire episode in the life of his family had a profound effect on the evolution of his attitudes towards marital sexuality. He would have rejoiced in the announcement early in 1959 that a branch of the Catholic Marriage Advisory Council was to be opened at George St. in Hull; and could well have had a hand in it. Well in advance of *Humanae Vitae* he came to believe that there was a proper role for contraception in a wholesome Catholic marriage; and said so after the encyclical appeared, not stridently but nonetheless clearly. Henceforward, he steadily enhanced his knowledge and refined his understanding of all aspects of sexuality and developed close working relations with professional experts in the field, such as Dr. Jack Dominian. His determination to patrol the cutting-edge of this aspect of moral theology bore rich fruit in his counselling over many years.

The other personal matter which pre-occupied him before, during and beyond these years was his continuing relationship with Mildred. Most of the surviving correspondence between them dates from Storey's period at St. Charles.

> During my time there in the centre of the city there were times when one got very depressed. I also was still very deeply in love with my friend and I used to get off whenever I could to see her and have a day together, but these were very tense times, especially as the work I was doing had me down sometimes.

In fact, they saw each other not only intermittently but rarely, partly because of the distance involved. Both were very busy – she taught those about to sit their 11+ and for years never had fewer than 50 pupils in her class. They took care to avoid gossip or scandal, meeting in isolated locations or, usually, as part of a large group. They had what they called their 'Union rules': never to talk by phone and only to write once a month on previously agreed feast days, though the latter was quite frequently broken.

Although by the time Storey arrived in Hull they had been close for seven or eight years, his appointment to St. Charles seems to have intensified their feelings. At Christmas 1958 M. celebrated the second anniversary of the day she 'got your first super letter, telling me all about us'; and six months later, having received a book from him, she wanted to write 'Feast of SS Peter and Paul 1957 in it....since – as you so beautifully put it – we first broke into each other's souls'. Worse than the physical distance between them was the difficulty of keeping a rein on their feelings on the few occasions when they were alone together. She suspected that Storey found this more challenging than she did. 'You, man that you are....find all this joy disturbing & so that *you*....may have peace of body, we'll just have to give up that sweet, spontaneous giving of lips and arms'. On the other hand there were limits to her own powers of self-denial. On one occasion, apparently after Storey had suggested that they further restrict their meetings:

> I say 'yes' with a full heart & mind to U[nion] R[ules] and no seeing, but I *couldn't* –not yet - say I'd not mind if I *never* saw you again until heaven. Sorry dear but I can't manage that.

Their quandary was probably made no easier by the advice received (and ignored) from Hilda, a friend of Mildred's and the only other person to know about their relationship: 'you would find it much easier if you saw more of each other'.

It was Storey who hit upon what became a chief means of communication between them.

I read Anne Frank's diary and realised she kept herself sane by writing a diary….I started writing a diary about all my thoughts and what was going on, and kept this for a long time. [I] used to send..[pages]..to my friend, my loved one, and this went on for about ten years.

Among his papers only a single extract from this diary has survived, for 18 August 1961, just after the end of a dock strike, and just before he left St. Charles.

Ships in the roads – how lovely and brave they are. I went to the riverfront to say my Office & draw, & it was high tide….Oh enormous great boats in the roads right down the river – tide up & so lock & dock gates. And bridges swinging to the hooting of the tugs' sirens as they edged giants in and out of the narrow gaps between the walls & towering keels slipped past within inches of where we stood. Flags & pennants, men shouting, wash swirling & the whole river alive. No Office got said.

Mildred warmly welcomed his efforts: 'yes please, I *do* want to read *all* your journal, and it won't be a bore to me'. And yet she was not slow to chide him when he became too cerebral for her. 'The notes on the 'Art of Loving' are alright, sweetheart, but you intellectual ones should remember that God himself is not a complex thing'.

Inevitably, Storey's greatest fear was that by continuing the relationship he was depriving Mildred of the husband and the children she might have. She on the other hand steadfastly maintained that she had no wish to marry. She derived huge satisfaction from her teaching career and beyond that was determined to care for her parents into their old age. There were times, however, when she too found it hard going.

Please pray to God for me that I might find in Him all the beauty and joy of fulfilment that would have been mine if He had willed that you and I be not 'as we are'. I'm finding it terribly hard just now.

This was in 1957, and it prompted Storey to write to her about his greatest fear. Her reply was prompt and unequivocal.

> Listen carefully to me, my A., you simply must stop these thoughts that are causing you so much pain. His Majesty's work will suffer if you go on, you know that, & I, as your dear love, cannot bear to think that this should happen. I want to help and not to hinder....I am *not* unfulfilled – a thousand times more fulfilled, content, at peace & full of joy than I have ever been....I'm all for His Majesty and my children are His – those He has given to me to guide and teach each year (all 52 of them) and I couldn't do that if I had to be busy feeding and clothing my own.

To judge from the language they used with each other, it was a relationship of equals.

At one stage, as a result of what Storey described as a 'mistake', they thought the housekeeper at St. Charles suspected they were very close, although nothing came of this. Nevertheless, Storey found the absence of any public acknowledgement of his love for Mildred especially painful. Regularly marooned in the centre of Hull, he longed not only 'for the hills and dales', but also 'for the *eternal* day when I shall be allowed to shout to all the world that I love you, and none shall despise us, or look askance'. Yet in the same letter, he returned, as he did periodically, to his great fear for Mildred.

> Though I would never dream of ever wanting you to be other than you are, yet if it did happen that Our Loves led you to find a fulfilling human love in some as yet undiscovered friend, you would never withhold your love on my account, would you? Oh, how I can *feel* your sweet wrath mounting as you read this; well, forgive me dear. I *do* have moments of terrible pull myself, but knowing that His Majesty has

commanded me to my post in His court, I find it fairly easy to 'come to heel' soon, and return to the deep happiness of your friendship in his work. But I don't feel that *you* are under that same clear command and vocation as that, and that therefore you may sometimes find loneliness too much.

Mildred's reply has not survived, but there is no reason to believe that it was any different from earlier ones, for their relationship, albeit largely at a distance, continued.

One reason for this was that they shared an extraordinary experience in 1958. Each had been to the Lady Shrine at Lourdes before then but, in that centenary year of Our Lady's apparitions, they took part in a diocesan pilgrimage, presided over by Bishop Brunner. 'Somewhat unwillingly', he recalled, Storey was one of several Assistant Chaplains, while Mildred went as one of a large group of lay pilgrims. At that point they had come, however reluctantly, to the conclusion that they should 'give up our closeness, which was a disturbance to us both, and a cause of anxiety, certainly': *unless* they received 'an outward sign of complete assurance that things weren't wrong'. So they both prayed for such a sign. In those pre-Conciliar days there was no concelebration of Mass by several priests. There were various private chapels for priests to use, but only one priest at a time could say Mass at the Lourdes Grotto. With numerous national groups seeking that opportunity, arrangements were complex and fraught. Moreover, it was regarded as a special privilege to be allowed to say Mass at the Grotto at midnight and, to the immense gratification of the Middlesbrough group, they were granted this privilege. The couple had prayed that Storey be given the chance to officiate at the Grotto at some point during that week. However:

the very next day the leader of the pilgrimage came up to me, just by chance it seemed, and said: 'Storey, you're the youngest priest on the pilgrimage and it's our night tonight to have the Grotto for our Midnight Mass. And so I've asked the Bishop and he suggests that you as the youngest priest should celebrate the Midnight Mass on the Grotto'. Which I did, and that was quite extraordinary....It was a great affirmation and it was such joy to both of us that it happened

And so their closeness continued, though there are few further details of the course of their relationship.

Towards the end of his life Storey paid tribute to how much he had gained from his relationship with Mildred, linking it, significantly, with his dealings with women in general.

This was love of desire like mad. With great help from friends it has been a great blessing for me, but I feel nobody gave me any preparation. She was just as vulnerable at her age of 21/22: no preparation at all of how to deal with it. It was an extraordinary experience; it was enriching the way I was able to be with people of the opposite sex.

He felt that in this respect above all his seminary training had been thoroughly inadequate. Subsequently, guided by what he had learned from Aelred and Fromm, he refused to insulate himself from half the human race. Unlike his brother, Peter, who had as little as possible to do with women, he remained open to them and to their friendship and affection. This attitude was grounded in his experience with Mildred, a strong and resourceful character who was even more adept than he was in managing their situation; and although they found it difficult, there is no doubt that they kept matters between them within proper bounds.

When she was near the end of her life she told me she thought the diary was too personal and too dangerous, and so she destroyed it. So I am rather sad that I lost so many of my notes of that time. But I think she was probably wise because there would have been upset and trouble, I suppose, if it had come into the open. But my relationship of love with her really did keep sound and was a great help during that time, so I just record that.

Mildred died in December 1985, aged 63. Storey kept a coloured photograph of her gravestone among his papers for the rest of his life.

Storey returned to Lourdes (together on some, if not all, occasions with Mildred) during each of the four years following the centenary, i.e. for as long as he remained at St. Charles. He went either as a chaplain or as a *brancardier* and she in an auxiliary nursing capacity. Particularly as a *brancardier*, responsible for sick people in wheelchairs or on stretchers, and mingling with many different nationalities, he 'began to realise… .what an enormous number of people there are in the world who suffer'. This experience fostered his subsequent deep engagement with issues of poverty and underdevelopment. It also set his feelings about conditions in inner-city Hull in a broader and more realistic perspective.

In the city progress was clearly evident by the turn of the 1950s. Most of the bomb damage had been repaired, slum clearance had proceeded apace, and the riverside quay, totally destroyed during the war, had been re-built. Fresh challenges were appearing: some trade never returned and the decline in dockwork, steep during the inter-war years, became even steeper; and with the advent of factory ships the fishing industry went into a decline which was soon made even sharper by the outcome of the Icelandic cod wars. Nonetheless, the poverty and squalor which had so shocked Storey on his arrival in Hull largely disappeared. Periodically, he continued to feel a personal need to escape from the city, which no doubt prompted some of his initiatives: arranging parish outings to Mount Grace, for example, and the organisation of an annual cricket match for parishioners at his family's old stamping ground in Everingham. Increasingly, however, this had more to do with his deep love of the landscape of his childhood than with conditions in the city.

Early in 1959 Storey's mother, Harriet, died and he passed his 40th birthday. He was in a reflective mood and a set of notes from August that year reveal some of the things on his mind. He regarded patience as a quality which he badly needed to cultivate. He must learn to bear with those who didn't interest him and (like Fr. Knowles, it seems) positively welcome those who intruded on his allocation of his own time. Particular circumstances required patience: 'rights will not be claimed when only personal to myself' and 'slights will *not* be more than momentarily resented'. He also recognised a need to be patient with himself 'in depression' and 'in failure, guilt and accidie'; and with both himself and God 'in loneliness'. His reflection on the maintenance of chastity was singular: 'never soothe with touch, however much it seems called for'. He wondered about his personal prospects. One of the things that Fr. Bob Dyson had warned students about at St. Mary's Hall was 'the danger of always wanting to change jobs'. Yet, in view of his hard and successful work at St. Charles, Storey could not help hoping for promotion from a curacy. A letter from his sister Patience in April 1960 appears to have been a response to his own feelings on the matter.

> I do wish you could get a parish. This waiting time is so hard and can't be meant to last forever. How long, O Lord, how long – one rather feels that. I certainly do about my own life.

In fact, change – of a different, unusual and challenging kind – was only just around the corner.

In addition to his duties at St. Charles, Storey was a regular, albeit infrequent, visitor to the University in Hull, which was situated outside the parish on the northern outskirts of the city. He was occasionally invited to speak in the Debates Union, attended other events from time to time, and facilitated the annual Mass at St. Charles's, held to mark the beginning of the academic year. A University Catholic Society, run by a committee of students, organised an annual programme of speakers and outings, and published an occasional magazine, *Veritas*. Many members went to Mass and had coffee on Saturday mornings in the Marist church near the campus. By the autumn of 1960, according to Kevin Connolly, then the President of the Society, students were 'immensely indebted to the local clergy and in particular to Fr. Storey, who annually makes an enormous impression upon all who listen to him'.

The University had originally been established as a College whose students took their degrees from the University of London. By the time it obtained its Charter in 1954, and with it the power to grant its own degrees, enrolment had grown to over 700. It continued to grow and by the start of the next decade had some 1,660 students. A Marist priest, Fr. Charles Howarth, served as Catholic Chaplain on a part-time basis. Bishop Brunner decided that this was inadequate for an institution of the University's size and significance. He himself was one of the few clergy in the diocese to have obtained a degree – at the University of Durham while resident at Ushaw; during his many years in Hull he had witnessed the growth of the University College; and he now decided that, from the autumn of 1962, Storey should leave St. Charles and become the University's first full-time Catholic Chaplain.

22: Storey on being appointed Catholic Chaplain at the University of Hull.

CHAPTER SEVEN

UNIVERSITY CHAPLAINCY 1962-72

Storey's appointment as Chaplain at Hull came at a key juncture in the life of the University and of British higher education as a whole. Hitherto, access to university education had been available only to an elite, amounting by the early 1960s to less than 5% of the post-school age-group. And yet, under the Education Act of 1944, an increasing proportion of pupils were staying on for sixth-form work and more of them were obtaining the qualifications required for university entrance. In addition. a post-war boom in births was scheduled to boost both trends. In February 1961 the government established a committee under the chairmanship of Lord Robbins to report and make recommendations about the issues arising from this situation. Its report was published in October 1963: via existing universities and the creation of new ones, it recommended a rapid expansion of higher education, from the 216,000 students of 1962-63 to some 390,000 students by 1973-74, and to 560,000 by 1980-8. The government accepted the Committee's recommendations and undertook to finance them.

A University College of Hull had been established at Hull in 1928 as an affiliate of London University and, like many other institutions, experienced severe difficulties during the war. It survived and grew slowly but steadily thereafter – to some 1,770 students in 1961-62. Managing the subsequent rapid expansion was not easy, requiring parallel growth in academic and support staff, and in buildings and other facilities. Of the 38 proposals for new physical developments at Hull across the decade or so from the early 1960s, 24 major projects were completed. By the mid-1970s, therefore, the main site on Cottingham Road in north Hull was 'reasonably full of buildings', whereas in 1962 there had been merely 5 or 6, along with temporary huts. Thus, Storey took up his new post just before the first period of major university expansion which led eventually, after many subsequent shifts in government policy, to the system of mass higher education that exists today.

Preparations for the appointment of a full-time chaplain had been underway for some time. While parish priest of St. Charles Bishop Brunner had hosted the High Mass celebrated during the first term of each academic year. Following his move to Middlesbrough he retained influential lay contacts in Hull through whom he initiated the earliest moves. Running a school close to the main campus, the Marists had done what they could to meet the pastoral needs of the students. Prompted by the bishop, Fr. Charles Howarth, the latest in a series of part-time Marist chaplains, convened the meeting on 24 January 1960 at which a Chaplaincy Association was formed, with Tom Farrell, one-time Sheriff of Hull, as Chairman and Kevin McNamara, the future M.P. for North Hull, as one of two Joint Secretaries.

The Association's immediate objective was to acquire a building for a Chaplaincy which, everyone agreed, had to be as close as possible to the University. Several properties were considered, and one was pursued as far as the auction room, only for the Association to be outbid. The task became urgent from the spring of 1962 when Bishop Brunner announced his intention of appointing a full-time chaplain from the autumn. The Association held its first General Meeting on 10 May 1962, by which time it was known that Storey was to be appointed. During the summer the Committee heard that 44, Newland Park was shortly to come on the market. This was a substantial Edwardian

23: The University Catholic Chaplaincy, 44, Newland Park, Hull, with the extension to the rear.

building on a sizeable plot, located in a quiet avenue a very short distance from the University. The house had been owned by an orthodox Jewish family, and there were wooden phylactories for scrolls with the *Shemah* inside them on every doorway. The Association obtained a grant in aid of purchase of £7,000 from the charitable trust founded by Francis Patrick Finn, a former Lord Mayor and Sheriff of Hull; and Storey moved in shortly after the beginning of term in October.

The impact on the life of many students was immediate. A full-time chaplain and counsellor suddenly became readily available. The quasi-domestic ambience of the Chaplaincy provided an alternative to the crowded communal facilities in the University. While a few students lived on the top floor, many more used the common room and library- cum-meeting room on the ground floor. Mass, which previously had been said once a week in the Sanctuary Hut on campus, was now said daily (including weekends) on the first floor of the Chaplaincy. The University Catholic Society had its own venue for the many events - meetings, talks, dances and parties - organised during the academic year. The new chaplain ensured from the outset that anyone and everyone, of whatever belief or none, was made welcome. Perhaps Storey's greatest achievement as Chaplain – undoubtedly bolstered by the fact that so many people in the University already knew him or of him – was that 44, Newland Park became another general venue at the University, and a highly popular one at that. While their particular needs were catered for, Catholic students, far from looking inwards, were encouraged to look outwards to the University as a whole and beyond.

Together with its popularity as a venue, the growth of student numbers after Robbins generated the need for an extension to the Chaplaincy and the back garden of 44, Newland Park provided ample space for one. Construction began in 1966 and the extension was opened on 21 January 1967 by the University Chancellor, Lord Middleton, by which time 3,327 students were enrolled at Hull. During the economic difficulties of the late 1960s the government reined back the rate of expansion, and by the end of Storey's decade as Chaplain total student numbers were just short of 4,000. The substantial two-storey extension ran straight out from the rear of the existing building. The whole of a split-level ground floor housed a large common room, including catering facilities and a bar. Upstairs there was space for a resident housekeeper, a guest bedroom, and an office; and a library and a chapel, separated by a partition which, when slid back, left the large area used for Mass on Sundays. The most striking feature of the chapel was a magnificent, if harrowingly stark, ceramic altar mural of the Crucifixion, specially commissioned by Storey from the Yorkshire artist Bob Brumby. The complex was impressive and eminently fit for purpose.

Forty-three years old and in his prime, Storey took up his responsibilities with zest. Much as he had thrown his energy and talents into his curacies and particularly enjoyed working with Fr. Knowles, he had hoped to be offered something more than a subordinate role. He now had one that he prized. Having hugely enjoyed Cambridge, he knew he was suited to life in a university and its regular contact with academics and students, its ferment of ideas and vibrant atmosphere. From the start Storey said he would give a decade of his life to the job, and he did so.

His start as Chaplain was nothing less than dramatic.

> It was during that very early time that I remember a nearby parish priest rang me and asked why were all the students going to Confession, had something upset them. And I said I don't know why, but actually it was the Cuban crisis....We all thought the end of the world was going to come. It was an extraordinary beginning....

Before long there were multiple startling new departures – in attitudes towards politics and public life; culturally, in music, film, theatre and the arts; and in personal behaviour and sexual mores.

> The Cuban crisis was just the beginning of all sorts of things....The effects of the Newport festival in America made such a difference to students. Joan Baez and Bob Dylan, [and] Peter Paul and Mary – that kind of folk singing, and at the same time the sudden appearance of Elvis Presley, the Rolling Stones and of course on top of that the Beatles, and the whole movement of life changed.

His experience of the 'sixties was far from unalloyed, but in retrospect his verdict was unhesitatingly positive: 'it was an extraordinary period and I lived a wonderful time....the 'sixties are a very great memory for me and deep friendships grew out of that'.

The start of his chaplaincy also coincided with the opening of the Second Vatican Council. Having been announced in January 1959 by a new Pope, John XXIII, it eventually got underway on 11 October 1962, just as Storey moved into 44, Newland Park. Loyal and utterly committed to the Church, he had nevertheless felt for years that it had lots of faults long overdue for repair and many avenues still to explore. He always hoped that the Council would seize the opportunity for reform and renewal, and he was not disappointed. As they proceeded, he found the deliberations of the Council exhilarating: they were reported promptly, sometimes sensationally but in general very reliably; he followed avidly the process whereby decrees emerged; and he shared his knowledge and views widely. It has been described, and he would have agreed, as 'the most revolutionary Christian event since the Reformation'.

While setting the tone for his chaplaincy, Storey's enthusiasm for the Council deeply influenced his outlook and ministry for the rest of his life. When first called,

> it was more or less in the control of a very right-wing, old-style Cardinal [Alfredo Ottaviani] who really wanted things to go on much the same. He wondered why the Pope was being so stupid in calling a Council. And when the bishops arrived they weren't going to wear [Ottaviani's judgement] and the whole thing had to be completely re-started. It was just fresh air; it was wondrous. Suddenly the Church seemed to be coming alive.

He regarded *Lumen Gentium,* the decree on the constitution of the Church, as

> perhaps the most important [decree] of them all. It recognised that the Church was primarily the people of God

and….not primarily the Pope and the Bishops. And when the people of God are called to do various tasks, they are all sharers in that priesthood of Christ.

The decree went far beyond the encyclical *Mystici Corporis* of two decades earlier, not merely in its re-assessment of the role of lay people, but also in its recognition of the spiritual reality of other Churches, and most particularly in its emphasis on collegiality in its treatment of the relationship between the episcopate and the papacy. Complementary to all this was the decree *Gaudium et Spes,* which endeavoured to reconcile Catholicism with the modern world after decades of institutional myopia. In seeking to discern the signs of the times, it proclaimed a wish to work with all men for the good of humanity.

For Storey there were at least three other highlights. Firstly, the decree on religious freedom: 'freedom to follow your conscience – one is bound to follow one's conscience, but one's conscience must be free, it may not be imposed on you'. Secondly, the decree on Ecumenism, which broke decisively with earlier rejections of the ecumenical movement. And finally, the decree on the Liturgy, which transformed Catholic worship, encouraging greater simplicity and lay participation, and introducing the use of the vernacular instead of Latin. There is overwhelming evidence of the influence of these developments on Storey's priestly ministry during the second half of his life: among many other instances, he never lost an opportunity as a parish priest to re-model his churches to facilitate the new liturgy; no-one in the diocese was more active ecumenically than he; and the last of his publications was entitled 'On Collaborative Ministry'. He was much heartened by the new Coadjutor Bishop of Middlesbrough, Gordon Wheeler, who 'asked to come to the University after each session [of the Council] and gave a lecture about what had been happening in Rome'. Along with other qualities, the fact that Storey was absolutely up-to-date with the

Council's progress won him the respect and admiration of both students, academic staff and lay people. And the buoyancy which he gained from this and the deliberations of the Council gave impetus to the discharge of his responsibilities.

At the outset there was some adjustment by both parties to the chaplain/student relationship. Hearing rumours that he was an intellectual heavyweight and confronted by his cut-glass, upper-class accent, some students, especially the 'freshers', found him somewhat intimidating. Until they encountered his sense of fun and his calm articulacy about the faith, they felt that he might be lofty and severe. For his part Storey found the mix of students very different from his experience at Cambridge - much younger, with far fewer mature students and many more women. He delivered two early series of talks, on 'The Problem of Man' and 'The Catholic Faith': but, unconvinced that this was the right approach and sensitive to fears that 44, Newland Park might become a 'glorified Youth Club', he then decided to leave the student-led Catholic Society to organise most events. The Society had a tradition of inviting Catholic public figures as speakers, which it further developed now it had its own premises and Storey's ideas and contacts to draw on. Previous successes, such as the journalists Hugh Kay of the *Catholic Herald* and Patrick O'Donovan of *The Observer,* were invited back, and among new guests were Storey's friend from Middlesbrough, Fr. Herbert McCabe, now at Blackfriars, Oxford, Walter Stein, the nuclear disarmer, from Leeds University, and the psychiatrist and marital theologian, Dr. Jack Dominian from the Maudsley Hospital in London, each of whom subsequently returned from time to time. For several years Storey limited his own set-pieces to the University Debates Union where, famously, he duelled with a Philosophy don, Axel Stern, in a debate on atheism and Christianity, with Storey (in cloth cap and corduroys) speaking in favour of the former, and Stern (in dark suit and clerical collar) the latter. While Stern, evoking considerable sympathy, was conscientious and straightforward, Storey spoke in such a way as to suggest that it would be impossible for anyone to believe a word he was saying. A mischievous but bravura performance was much admired that day and for long afterwards.

As time went on programmes became steadily more diverse and adventurous. One group went to a conference in Cambridge in 1965; there was a visit to a Borstal in 1967; and a pilgrimage to Iona at Easter 1971. At Storey's personal invitation in the mid-'sixties a local witch came to the Chaplaincy to explain her beliefs. The poet, Philip Larkin, the University Librarian who was also jazz critic of the *Daily Telegraph,* was disinclined to speak publicly about poetry - he said that poems 'just came to him' - but he twice accepted invitations from Storey to talk about jazz and play a selection of his records. By the Spring of 1972, shortly before the end of Storey's time, speakers included Guy Stringer, Chairman of Oxfam, Arthur Watts on 'Gypsies', Peter Hebblethwaite on 'Justice', Peter Moloney, a teacher, Scouse wit and T.V. host, and the lay theologian Rosemary Haughton. By that stage Catholic Society events attracted such large numbers that they were often held in the Students' Union: with Sally Trench, the heroine of down-and-outs, Fr. Arthur McCormack, a Vatican theologian, on the population explosion, Gratton Puxon of the Gypsy Council, and Dom Ian Petit, a charismatic Benedictine from Ampleforth, who spoke in tongues. By then too Storey himself was regularly putting himself about. He obliged one group who asked for a Mass in French and gave lectures in the Drama Department on the ritual of the Mass. Eventually, according to one student, the Catholic Society became 'the largest Union Society and certainly the most varied in its programme'. In another opinion, 'the number and variety of people passing through the Chaplaincy at various times was exceeded only by the Union building itself'. One visitor during

24: The Chapel on the first floor of the Chaplaincy extension, with Bob Brumby's Altarpiece.

this later period was Storey's History teacher from Stonyhurst, Christopher (now Sir Christopher) Hollis.

While Storey was undoubtedly influential in these developments, it was a relatively insubstantial element in his work, much of which involved dealing with individuals on a personal basis. With many students having recently become independent for the first time, it was in the nature of university life to pose problems which they had to solve or at least learn to cope with. And whether or not this was achieved, there gradually loomed the question of precisely what they were going to do with the rest of their lives. By common consent among those who knew him as Chaplain, Storey was a skilled counsellor: a good listener; a shrewd judge of personality; sufficiently experienced to estimate the relative severity of the problems which were encountered; with a host of professional contacts who might, if necessary, be pointed to or called on; and disinclined to dictate, preferring instead to guide a student to his/her own solution. Yet all this would have been to little avail had he not won the confidence of the student community. He did this by immersing himself in their way of life. Other than in most unusual circumstances, he attended everything that was organised in the Chaplaincy and much that took place outside it.

> He displayed….an almost saint-like disregard for his own possessions and position, ready, at the drop of a hat, to welcome a beggar, provide food and to offer his own coat (literally) to those in need.

Above all, he was constantly available, from early in the morning, often until early in the following morning.

Immersion was well-nigh total. At weekends he lost no opportunity of getting into the countryside, usually the Wolds, occasionally stopping for refreshment with one of the many farming families he knew, but invariably with students in tow. If he had to visit a parish in the diocese on a weekday evening, he often took students with him, dropping them off somewhere to amuse themselves before rendezvousing once his work was done. During the early years he gave absolute priority to activities with students, once turning down an invitation to lunch with the Vice-Chancellor in favour of joining students on a visit to Rievaulx. During Christmas and Easter vacations there were longer and more adventurous trips, often to the Lake District, one at Easter to climb the Cuillins on Skye, and another at New Year to tackle Ben More in the Highlands. Summer excursions were usually longer and one year included some weeks in northern Italy, visiting the fifth-century mosaics in Ravenna and climbing the Marmolada in the Dolomites; and, after returning via Cologne (over which Gerard Storey's plane had been shot down), viewing Charlemagne's treasure in Aachen. By being so persistently in the company of students Storey kept his finger on the pulse of their attitudes and opinions, while they, with the opportunity of getting to know him extremely well, came to regard him with great respect and affection.

His core activity as Chaplain – saying Mass and preaching – left a deep impression on those who saw and heard him. According to one student, 'when I witnessed him saying Mass or giving a sermon, it often seemed to me that I was witnessing a man who was being transported on to a spiritual plane inaccessible to me'. There was generous eye-contact with all those participating and the celebration proceeded at a pace whereby each word, gesture and episode was given due emphasis. Frequently adopting an historical approach to Scripture, his preaching was educative, and its tone was informal and conversational. He was often topical, picking up on recent developments or forthcoming events; he referred to books or articles that had impressed him; and he came to clear conclusions. The qualities which characterised his writing and public speaking elsewhere were brought into the chapel.

Storey was a great success as Chaplain and soon made his mark beyond Hull, being invited to succeed Monsignor Gilbey as Chaplain at Cambridge. His bishop declined to release him, but it was no surprise when in 1969 he was elected Chairman of the University Catholic Chaplains in Britain for his last three years. When he retired from Hull he was elected unanimously as National Chaplain of the Catholic Students' Council.

It is clear nevertheless that his decade at the University fell into two contrasting halves. The first five years were ones of hectic growth in student numbers and facilities, one of the latter being the Chaplaincy itself. Storey's job stretched him, but he also found it exciting and at times exhilarating. During the next five years, when growth continued but more slowly, and then tailed off, he detected a change of atmosphere: buoyancy gave way to uncertainty and aimlessness. Then, during the student troubles of 1968, which were severe in France, Germany, the U.S.A. and Britain, there developed a fear of anarchy as student protests brought work in some institutions, including Hull, to a virtual standstill. During Storey's last two years a combination of factors – exhaustion through overwork, renewed student unrest, and a serious car accident – reduced him to a low point from which he fully recovered only after leaving the Chaplaincy.

Writing to a friend in December 1967 before the onset of the student troubles, he outlined early misgivings about developments.

Landmarks seem to be in flux & some seem to be tumbling altogether….At the University here this weekend there are to be three days of 'experimental theatre'- a sort of anti-theatre. Anti-conventional dancing, underground films, juxtaposition of the beautiful and the bizarre & and all the conventions blown up….Now what is it about? And why? It is revolt, rejection, making laughter of what? Against whom? And to what end? I just don't know. I feel alienated from my fellow old-style priests who don't even try to understand….& more and more alienated from the student world. They no longer talk a language or live a life that I am at home with….Reports seem to indicate this is not confined to my rather precious student world….

I have just about finished 25 years as a priest & looking back there is much that has changed in my own way of thinking and acting but, oh boy, the old Mass is still, every day, the splendid classic of what life is about….Little else of the 'paraphernalia' of the Church matters a toss. For those to whom it does matter & is a *help,* well and good, but it doesn't *worry* me to think that old Mrs. O'Boyle will get to heaven on her unceasing rosary etc. Must stop – lots to *talk* about.

Storey's firecracker letters were eagerly anticipated by his many correspondents. From now on, however, they frequently demonstrated his capacity to move from deep gloom to firm conviction in a few sentences. As with this one, many of them also illustrate that, while he was always eager for a discussion, he challenged students when he encountered among them confusion, lack of discipline and the absence of principle.

There was a great deal more for him to worry about during 1968. Student protests occurred in various parts of the world, some about purely local problems and others about much broader issues, such as apartheid, the nuclear threat and the war in Vietnam. Prominent locations were Los Angeles, Berlin and Paris; and in Britain there was repeated agitation over the appointment of Walter Adams (previously Vice-Chancellor and Principal of the University College of Southern Rhodesia) to the Directorship of the London School of Economics. During 1968 British protests spread to the Hornsey College of Art and the universities in Cambridge, Essex, Exeter, and Leicester: and to Hull where, on 30 May, a meeting of the Socialist Society in the Students' Union was held 'to express solidarity with the French students [and]....and their struggle in Paris....against the authoritarian nature of the education in France'. The meeting proceeded to identify eight features of authoritarianism in the system at Hull, including issues as diverse as examinations, communications, fees, grants, secrecy, catering, and the issue of the University acting 'in loco parentis'. A large body of students walked across campus to occupy the Administration Building where, refusing the offer of the Vice-Chancellor Brynmor Jones of a private meeting with their representatives, they held a public discussion with him and some senior colleagues in the entrance hall. The students were eventually persuaded to disperse, but only after the Vice-Chancellor had agreed to discuss the 'eight points' further at a meeting of students and members of the University

Senate.

With the academic year far advanced students were fearful of delaying tactics and set about selecting their representatives and consolidating arguments underpinning their eight points. Attendance at their meetings grew, with 700 on 31 May and around 1,000 on 4 June when the Union assumed overall leadership. The Vice-Chancellor repeatedly indicated that no single member of the Senate, not even himself, could ratify changes not duly considered in the Committee system; and that some of the issues were beyond the Senate's remit. Nevertheless, on 6 June the Senate set up a joint committee of itself and the Union Council to consider matters. While many at the student meeting on the following day regarded this as a delaying tactic, a motion to stage a sit-in immediately was defeated by 312 votes to 267. At a joint meeting of the two bodies on 8 June the question of student representation in the committee system predominated. Towards the end of a long working day it was agreed, though not unanimously, to set up a series of parallel staff/student committees across the University: but when this decision returned to the Union meeting which followed, it was rejected. A sit-in began at once, severely disrupting the University's routine at one of the busiest times of year. Eventually, on 12 June some 1,500 attended a joint meeting of staff and students, voting by 818 to 635 to end the sit-in; and next day matters began to return to normal.

This sequence of events was reported widely and sensationally in the local and national press. It was unprecedented in the history of the institution and shook it to the core. According to Storey,

> at the University it was a very moving time. You were really on one side or the other. It was an absolute clash and the University was really in shreds about this. Nothing else was talked about at all.

Nor did 1968 see the end of such difficulties. During the next session, hampered by both inquorate and inconclusive meetings, final agreement on the arrangements for staff/student committees proved elusive and ultimately they were instituted for an experimental period only. Further problems arose in 1971 with the national agitation over apartheid. The University became involved through its holdings in the firm of Reckitt and Colman, which had South African connections and whose shares had been part of the original University endowment. Meetings of some 2,000 – 2,500 students were involved and there was a further occupation of the Administration block. After twelve days this ended when the issue was referred to a joint committee.

In March 1972, after the end of the second sit-in, all seven University chaplains issued a joint statement in which they were severely critical of the manner in which these episodes had developed.

> An issue arises with an accompanying feeling of injustice…
> .the matter reaches a Union meeting. The signals are given…
> .but it is our experience that signals go unheeded by the majority of students and by staff ….A sit-in consequently finds the vast majority of staff and students in helplessness and anger. Staff divides and polarises. Angry things are said and rumours abound. A Union meeting is next called, and this time it will be well over the thousand mark and the issue is discussed before a wide audience for the FIRST TIME. In this debate all the preparation is on one side, and any opposition to militant action is seen as square, reactionary, negative and cowardly….The sit-in becomes official policy by a huge majority.

Given his standing among the chaplains, there is little doubt that Storey played a leading part in formulating this statement. There is explicit testimony as to his broader role in events. One student's memory of the first episode recalled Storey's 'stand during the sit-in'; another wrote of Storey 'helping to quell, for a second time, the raging flames of a sit-in with the cool water of reason'. Events undoubtedly left their mark on him. He felt that, if he had his time over again, he would switch focus. On arrival as Chaplain he had decided that 'his first duty lay towards the Catholic students'; he eventually came to believe that his first duty was 'to the University itself'.

There was another major pre-occupation. In 1968, while all this was proceeding, Pope Paul VI issued his encyclical *Humanae Vitae*. After forbidding discussion of birth control at the Vatican Council, he had delegated the matter to an Advisory Commission. Although the Commission recommended change, the encyclical endorsed the Church's traditional teaching, provoking widespread disagreement. Like most people, Storey had expected change. He heard the news on the radio while travelling to the Hebrides with students, 'and we discussed it for the whole of the rest of the day'. The matter scarcely left his mind for many months and he summarised his views in a draft article, sending it to his bishop with a request for advice. The reply said it would be unhelpful to publish for the time being; the piece was never published.

Acknowledging that a conscientious Pope had taken the burden of decision-making entirely upon himself, Storey argued that:

> Marriage is the one sacrament of which the laity are the ministers, and therefore, it is said, the Spirit's utterance through the Christian married laity should have carried greater weight….the official Church still fails to recognise that truth….grows from within the Christian community, expressing what has been called the *sensus fidelium*.

The problem at the heart of the encyclical, he said, was that:

Once you declare that any contraceptive action is intrinsically wrong, i.e. objectively and in itself, then you are saying there can never be a situation where it is morally right….[The Pope] has, however, made it clear that this is not one of those supreme *ex cathedra* statements which we would term infallible. And so it follows logically [that] the Pope is admitting that his teaching in this matter is fallible.

This provided an opportunity for individuals to appeal to their conscience, but this, he argued, was of little comfort to many ordinary people.

Storey then moved on to what he felt had been largely ignored, but which, in his view, was 'more important in the days ahead'. Until relatively recently people had married somewhat later and died earlier, though not generally before at least some of their children. Now, he argued, a family of six would be an 'optimum maximum', and even with an average of four, population growth would be excessive; and the Church maintained that such social considerations, together with personal and family needs, should be borne in mind by parents. Moreover, it was only now, he maintained, that the relational and affective aspects of marriage were being deeply explored by theologians as well as by psychologists: 'the full richness of this has now led us to put this on a level with, and no longer secondary to, the procreation of children'. In fact, in paragraph 9, in 'one of the most beautiful and rich paragraphs in the whole encyclical', the unitive aspect of marriage was given 'clear priority over procreation'. 'The Christian's duty at a time like this', he concluded, 'is prayer and some hard thinking: it is not a time for breaking heads or hearts'.

As indicated earlier, Storey's convictions in this matter were powerfully influenced by the experience of his own parents. 'This had been on our minds as a family….for years'. Not only were there seven children, but also 'I think one or two miscarriages'.

As protests grew, he worked out his own position. By early September 1968, if the English bishops were to insist that:

we must accept [the encyclical] as a disciplinary decree & put it into practice, then I will have to ask to be 'stood down' for the present (& perhaps I would go off & do a year or two overseas) & hope for further light. But in conscience I cannot see that use of contraceptive aids in certain (not that few) cases I know of, & have to advise, is 'intrinsically' wrong and therefore sinful. Actually I feel we have no need to worry - *too* many bishops and theologians are disturbed also for it to rest. And the 'sense of the Church' will out.

And so it has proved.

Without being strident or combative, Storey remained open in his attitude towards this issue for the rest of his life, and counselled accordingly. He was sorely distressed by the Church's attempt to close down all discussion of the matter, which ran clean counter to his personal *modus operandi*: a philosophical or theological problem had to be thought right through; this demanded discussion with one's peers, perhaps over a very long period, and to forbid this was negative and damaging.

The whole idea of the marriage bed and that you're not meant to be making love except at a time when it is safe, which is about three to five days in the month when it's really completely safe….that makes a nonsense of having a marriage bed….Certainly the scriptural background does seem to me not to be opposed to it. But the arguments will go on and I'm afraid that for a great, great number of young people it's simply got no meaning at all. And if they are trying to love one another, I think the Church could give them so much guidance and the recognition of the importance of trying to have wholeness in one's marriage relationship.

167

He felt that it was essential for the matter to be opened up for discussion – 'of both sexes, not just of men only, and celibate men at that'; not to do so incurred 'a loss of the sense of the authenticity of the Church's teaching'.

The other issue which gave Storey major pause for thought towards the end of his chaplaincy was the attitude of the Church and his fellow clergy towards the then current expansion of higher education. This came to a head in 1970 when one of his diocesan colleagues, a much younger priest who was keen to pursue further studies in theology, was offered a place at the University of Oxford. When the diocese's initially positive attitude gave way to hesitation, Storey wrote, apparently to the Vicar General, urging 'special consideration'. His comments in support of granting leave were cast much wider than the individual context. He began by acknowledging that there were not many priests 'to play chess with' in filling parish vacancies. Yet 'higher studies, and our sharing in the ever growing world of Catholic graduate life', should not be regarded as an 'optional extra'. Twenty-seven years earlier he had been the last priest from the diocese of Middlesbrough to go to University. He could think of no other body 'of supposedly educated men, engaged largely in an educative task', that would have that record. Nor did he believe that any other English diocese was as backward in this regard as his own. 'I am myself regarded by many of the clergy as one of those "intellectuals" and quite overtly spoken of as a threat and a danger'. In his view many of his colleagues were afraid of 'the fantastic movements in world knowledge which our laity are sharing in, and our clergy hardly at all'.

And, to be honest, is it not one of the marks of the secular clergy that all of us to some extent, and the younger men especially, have a real inferiority complex when asked to join with, let alone give any lead to, graduate groups such as doctors, social workers, Newman etc? The fields of Social

Sciences and Theology are particular areas where our laity are increasingly leaving us on a level where we are in no position to lead them.

These forthright remarks reveal him in sombre mood as he approached the end of his time as Chaplain. He felt that he had done a reasonably good job, but that it had been largely in isolation and mistakenly regarded by several other priests as tangential to the core work of the diocese. He felt less than comfortable with some of his fellow clergy, and he knew that they felt likewise with him. This was dispiriting, and in sharp contrast to his relationship with the laity. He enjoyed excellent relations with all manner of lay people; by no means only, but especially, with those who particularly valued his intellectual capacity – as someone who was well-qualified, up-to-date, loved debate and would respond rationally and fluently to whatever they cared to throw at him. The change in his attitudes was also influenced by his much closer relations with University staff during his later years as Chaplain, not least with the beleaguered Vice-Chancellor, Brynmor Jones. Storey joined him on the Religious Affairs Committee and the two regarded each other with growing respect and warmth.

On 9 May 1972 Storey had a serious car accident. Testimonies to the poor quality of his driving, particularly *vis-a-vis* traffic lights, are legion: 'his driving could be terrifyingly reckless'; but in this case the cause appears to have been extreme tiredness. Driving from Hull to Holderness, he fell asleep at the wheel, shot across the road, narrowly missing oncoming traffic, and ended up deep in a ditch. In Accident and Emergency in Hull he was treated for shock and a badly fractured nose, and kept in hospital for a week. The calls on his time were resumed as soon as he was released, so a friend took him to Whitby for a week; and then on to his cousin, Helen Gillow and her husband at

Leighton Hall, near Carnforth, Lancashire where he stayed for a further week. By the time he returned to Newland Park examinations were well underway and things were quieter in the University. There were various farewell events before he set off on a recuperative summer trip, catching up with friends in various parts of Britain.

According to those who saw him regularly during this period, he suffered intermittently from depression for up to two years before he left the chaplaincy, brought on primarily by physical exhaustion which, in turn, stemmed from his 'endless availability: he could never say no to a request, callers, phone calls, tension mounting'. The accident made matters much worse and he began to react very adversely to all kinds of bad news, whether the condition of the man in the next hospital bed, the wilful damage done to Michaelangelo's *Pieta* in St. Peter's in May 1972, or the latest episode in the Vietnam War. On returning to the chaplaincy he learned that a deaf student whom everyone knew well had died of an overdose. 'He said Mass for him straight away and could hardly pronounce the words for crying'. His spirits were somewhat restored following his stay at Leighton Hall.

On 26 June fourteen Catholic staff in the University gave Storey lunch, expressing the 'respect and admiration' which they and their non-Catholic colleagues had for his work among them.

> Both in what you have done and in what you are, you have borne witness in a world accustomed to high standards of debate and given evidence of signal dedication, always and everywhere… Wherever you go, our good wishes go with you.

On 7 July, at a graduation ceremony in Hull City Hall, the Revd. A.T. Hanson, Professor of Theology in the University, presented Storey for the degree of Bachelor of Divinity, *honoris causa.*

Although he summarised Storey's education and experience before his appointment as Chaplain, lauding his development of 44, Newland Park, his contributions to the University Theological Society and his ecumenical activity, Professor Hanson insisted that the honour was bestowed:

> much more because of the sort of person he has shown himself to be during these past ten years. Everyone who comes into contact with him finds a sympathy, a humility, an honesty, an openness which witness clearly to the absolutely authentic quality of his Christianity. I do not think I know anyone who, while maintaining an unhesitating loyalty to his own Church, is more straightforward and honest about its shortcomings, and less inclined to make claims for it which cannot be substantiated. If ever anyone commended his Church by means of his life, it is Anthony Storey.

It was a rich tribute.

Rich, but not entirely unexpected. On the other hand, the *festschrift* entitled *The Greatest Storey,* with which past and present members of the University Catholic Society presented him, was entirely unprecedented. This collection of prose and poetry, art and photography contained remarkable tributes. Finding no other vehicle for her thoughts, Eva Pinthus, Warden of the University's Cleminson Hall in Cottingham (originally Lady Nun's summer residence), made her contribution here too. She described Storey's task, 'though by no means his only one', as 'guide, comforter, counsellor, stimulator, encourager, teacher, father confessor and friend'. He was 'incapable of doing anything by halves'. All were 'equally welcome, equally well looked after [and] credentials were never needed'. According to one student, Peter Crisell, Storey's 'contribution to generations of students of all persuasions [was] unique'. What Fred Case:

learned from Father Storey was the respect of myself and the affirmation of my values whilst respecting the rights of others. I can only hope that the thousands of students who have come into contact with him....have learned as much from him as I have done.

And for Ray Kinsella, 'it will be *something* to have been at Hull University in the years of Father Storey'.

CHAPTER EIGHT
STOKESLEY, BROUGH PARK
& BEDALE 1972-81

If the end of his University chaplaincy was a high point in Storey's growing reputation as a priest and counsellor, it was a low point in his health and spirits. His successor, Fr. Peter Keeling, whom he had taught years earlier at St. Joseph's Primary School on the Grove Hill estate in Middlesbrough, found him exhausted and depressed. Fortunately, Storey was granted leave during which he was able to re-charge his batteries. He had longed for a period of peace and quiet, undisturbed by calls on his time, and with people who shared his interests; and, having successfully completed probation as a teacher of religious education at St. Mary's School, he decided to catch up with the latest developments in the subject. From the late summer of 1972 till early 1973 he enrolled at the Institute of Religious Education at Corpus Christi College in London, 'feeling the need to listen and write and exchange and be renewed'. The Institute had recently been launched by the English hierarchy to educate priests and laity along the lines of the Belgian Lumen Vitae Institute. While there Storey again found himself in the congenial company of Fr. Hugh Lavery of the diocese of Hexham and Newcastle, earlier his contemporary at the English College and St. Mary's Hall, Stonyhurst. The two had much in common intellectually, not least their enthusiasm for Vatican II, and Fr. Lavery had been appointed to Corpus Christi to assist the Principal, Monsignor Michael Keegan. Despite the management's best efforts, the Institute was short-lived, not least because Cardinal Heenan, Archbishop of Westminster, was unimpressed by what he regarded as the radical theology taught there. However, Storey enjoyed his sabbatical and emerged certificated and refreshed.

His next appointment was his first as a Parish Priest - at St. Joseph's in Stokesley, a market town south-west of Middlesbrough. In addition to the parish church, there was a Mass Centre dedicated to St. Margaret Clitherow at nearby Great Ayton. His predecessor was none other than his brother, Peter. At the time this seemed a happy sequence, but that was not how matters turned out.

They had interests as well as experiences in common. It was Peter who, in the face of parental scepticism, supported his younger brother in testing his vocation. Both were committed environmentalists: being brought up in George Snowden Storey's household at Warter had ensured that. They had also spent some years together at the English College. Later, in addition to both serving as chaplains to the Student Cross pilgrimage to Walsingham in 1948, they shared a deep commitment to the pilgrimage shrine of the Lady Chapel at Mount Grace. As a newly-ordained priest in Middlesbrough Peter had discovered this site, overgrown and neglected, whilst on a weekend cycle ride with a fellow curate. Storey came to share his enthusiasm and, with Peter, did much to promote the shrine throughout the diocese. It was largely through their efforts that the Lady Chapel eventually became the diocese's major Marian shrine, which it remains. The most extensive of Storey's tree plantings lie on a hillside next to the lane leading to the shrine, a sure sign of his commitment to the place.

And yet in outlook the two men were very different. Peter was conservative to the core; steeped in the age-old Catholic traditions of northern England; sceptical, liturgically and intellectually, of many of the outcomes of Vatican II; and with a reputation as a misogynist. One parishioner, who with her husband-to-be turned up for a pre-marriage talk with Fr. Peter, maintained that her future parish priest failed to acknowledge, speak to or even look at her throughout the so-called discussion, dealing exclusively with her partner. Peter had as little to do with women as possible, which was perhaps his way of dealing with mandatory celibacy. More than enough has been said already to indicate how different this was from his younger brother's approach. According to one senior, retired priest of the Middlesbrough diocese, who knew both men (and the parish of St. Joseph's) very well, 'there was a vast difference' between the two; and the sharp contrast between them was possibly more obvious in the absence of a curate at St. Joseph's – each was on his own. It was against this background that Storey embarked on what turned out to be a difficult period.

In 1974, within a year or so of his arrival, the parish suffered a major catastrophe. St. Joseph's Church was very severely damaged by a fire caused by an electrical fault. Storey was out and about when the conflagration started.

Some three miles out on the Thirsk road, I first saw the strange white and dark mixture of steam and smoke rising in the mercifully windless, evening sky over Stokesley. With that strange instinct of our animal nature I felt a lump rising in my throat – the location and the distance from the town centre were too awfully certain. The horror of turning past the bridge into Meadowfield and seeing the fire-engines drained all feeling. The policeman let my car through the cordon and as I opened my car door my little dog ran off, tail down, into the dark across the fire hoses. 'You can't go in Father, it's a furnace in there and the electricity is still on', said a fire officer. I tried the sacristy door in order to get to the tabernacle, but a fireman halted me as the bellying red and black cloud burst out – and we slammed the door.

Minutes later - it seemed an hour – the power was cut off, and simultaneously the firemen broke in windows and doors. It was all over and in control in another hour – a sodden, smouldering, blackened shell.

It was a shocking setback which in due course he attempted to turn to positive use.

In his article for the diocesan *Directory* Storey underplayed the drama of the incident as far as he personally was concerned. In order to rescue the Blessed Sacrament he, clad in protective clothing, was carried into the blazing building by a fireman, who must have been a very strong fireman indeed. There was much that could not be saved. The high-pitched roof, paintings, statuary and furniture were destroyed: but, owing to the skill of the firemen, much beautiful glass was saved. Lots of practical help and support came from the local community, and other churches offered temporary accommodation and financial assistance. Bishop McClean (who had succeeded both Brunner, who had retired in 1967, and Gordon Wheeler, who had been translated to Leeds) opened a restoration fund in November 1974.

For Storey the fire was in one respect a blessing in disguise, providing an opportunity to turn a long, thin church into a church more in the round in the spirit of Vatican II. A vociferous group of parishioners advocated a straightforward re-instatement of what had been destroyed, but after vigorous engagements the arguments for a new order were accepted though, in certain quarters, slowly and reluctantly. Storey's most imaginative personal contribution was to get a local farmer to use his tractor in bringing a large, free-standing stone down from the moors to be the new altar. Bob Brumby, creator of the very moving altarpiece at the University Chaplaincy, then Deputy-Principal of York College of Art, was also involved, being responsible, among other things, for new door handles for the church, as was Helen Gillow, an interior designer and Storey's cousin. St. Joseph's was

25: Storey in the re-ordered church of St. Joseph's, Stokesley.

among the first churches in the diocese to be re-ordered to facilitate the new liturgy. While patient with those who disagreed with him, this was one area where Storey was reluctant to give way in the face of opposition.

Having already introduced annual financial accounts for the parish (welcomed by the laity, if not by all his fellow clergy), he went on to establish a Parish Council whose members were chosen via a simple electoral system. Parishioners could nominate themselves or others, and nominees were asked to provide a brief background statement and a photograph for display in the church porch. The Council had four to six members, including a Secretary, and met monthly. Parishioners were encouraged to submit questions or suggestions to it, and minutes of meetings were published in the parish bulletin. On the whole these arrangements worked satisfactorily and were continued by Storey's two immediate successors. In contrast his introduction of girl altar servers was short-lived, ending abruptly for reasons which are uncertain but which probably reflected opposition in some quarters.

One of his initiatives - the formation of a Third World Group at St. Joseph's – was of lasting value not merely to the parish but to the diocese. Soon after its foundation in 1962 he became a lifelong member of Amnesty International. Storey was always exercised by global problems such as poverty, underdevelopment and human rights, and became increasingly well-informed about them. At the University he had broadened the agenda of the Catholic Society to include such matters. At Stokesley each member of the Third World Group, which met monthly, was asked to deliver in their turn a short talk on a developing country, a region, or a particular commodity. This was a painless way of expanding the group's collective knowledge, and of identifying links between world trade, development issues and justice. The group also organised an annual sponsored walk (with Storey always covering the route in advance) to raise funds for CAFOD, thereby including parishioners of all ages even if they did not attend group meetings. After Storey left St. Joseph's the Stokesley group amalgamated with individuals from Holy Name parish in Middlesbrough, and were sufficiently well organised to be able to offer accommodation, furniture and other help to some Chinese boat people who fled Vietnam. The larger group formed the core of the diocesan Justice and Peace Commission which was set up by Bishop McClean's successor, Bishop Harris, in the early 1980s, of which Storey was the first Chairman, and which continues today.

One feature of the Third World Group at Stokesley was that it was open to non-Catholics. Along with his wish to extend the role of the laity in all aspects of parish life, a hallmark of all his service as a Parish Priest was his openness to people of other faiths. This had been strongly fostered in the University where he worked as one member of a large interdenominational team.

Quakers, for example, would attend his Masses at the Chaplaincy, and out of respect for their emphasis on silent worship, there would be an extended period of silence after Communion. At Stokesley various annual events took place with other churches and religious groups, among them a trip to the Holy Land with several of his Jewish friends. Canon David Smith, later Anglican Rector of Whitby, was his neighbour in Stokesley and left a particularly warm tribute.

> I know that I am one of many, many clergy and ministers who have valued the love and friendship that Tony Storey gave. I was serving…. in…. Stokesley in the early seventies when he arrived as the Parish Priest. I was never allowed to walk past the Presbytery but he insisted that I had to call in and say hello, pass the time of day and regale him with any gossip that he didn't already know! Over the next few years I grew to regard him as not only a brilliant Parish Priest but also as a confidant and friend. If I had time on a Sunday between services I would go and listen to Tony's sermons. They were always 'filled with good things' and the Love of God always shone out of both him and his words.

As far as ecumenism was concerned, Storey led powerfully by example.

Canon Smith had one vivid memory.

> I remember going into his church after the liturgical changes due to Vatican II were about to take place. Tony was telling his congregation that 'from next Sunday we are all going to pass the peace to each other. This is very easy and best done with a smile and a handshake'. Then, eyeballing some of his more elderly and holy ladies, he said with a twinkle in his eye: 'of course, if you think the person sitting next to you is a bit of a bastard, don't bother!' At that point I decided to leave before Anglican/R.C. relations took a dive through my

26: Monsignor Peter Storey.

laughter.

At first this may have been regarded as a joke which, in part, it certainly was. On the other hand, faced with some parishioners who with their former parish priest had grown sceptical of the changes, it was also perhaps an incentive in case, when it came to the point, their immediate neighbours misinterpreted their lack of action!

In late 1978 Storey was asked to move from Stokesley with effect from mid-1979. After six years there was nothing obviously untoward about this – secular priests were bound by obedience to serve the needs of their diocese, which were unpredictable. However, his posting was to a veritable backwater, the parish of St. Paulinus at Brough Park, near Catterick, which had a very small congregation and where Mass was said only occasionally; and the letter announcing this decision came from his brother, Peter, who was now a Canon, a Monsignor and, recently, a Vicar General. Moreover, Bishop McClean had died in August 1978 and his successor, Bishop Harris, was not appointed till November: and as Provost of the diocese Peter was in charge during this *sede vacante*.

According to the senior diocesan priest quoted earlier, it was felt that aspects of Storey's approach in Stokesley 'did not fit in'. Appointment to Brough Park constituted a 'dark night' of his soul; he knew that his brother was critical both of his attitudes and of his changes (some of which, it was suggested, had been introduced prematurely), as well as of the manner in which he carried out parts of his work. Although the decision led to vigorous protests from some parishioners at St. Joseph's, Storey was regarded by others, and by some of his fellow clergy, as 'too political': aspects of his approach at Stokesley had provoked misgivings among some parishioners; and for those who thought that the practice of Catholicism was primarily about personal salvation, the emphasis on lay involvement in parish affairs, on ecumenism, and on the problems of the third world, not to mention his re-ordering of the church, were too many steps too far. In sympathy, his successor at St. Joseph's, Fr. Leo Dennett, felt that Storey had been 'sent into the wilderness'. Storey himself was distressed and maintained that at first he felt 'like a leper'.

His subsequent situation at the church of St. Paulinus at Brough Park was somewhat reminiscent of his days at Everingham shortly after his ordination in 1943. While Everingham had been the home of the recusant Constable family, Brough Park had since penal days been the seat of the Catholic Lawson family. At Everingham the church of SS. Mary & Everilda had been built on the estate immediately after the Catholic Emancipation Act. William Lawson built the church of

St. Paulinus at Brough Park a few years later in 1837: it too was designed by an Italian, Ignatius Bonomi. The similarities, however, went no further. Members of the Norfolk family continued to live at Everingham Hall for years after George Storey's time and, although eventually sold by them, the Hall remains a family home to this day. Having already proved inconvenient for family life before the war, Brough Hall suffered severely from military occupation during it; and eventually came into the possession of the Worthington family. By the time of Storey's appointment they had sold it and gone to live in a smaller property on the estate, and the Hall had been converted into apartments.

In contrast to the church at Everingham, the church of St. Paulinus at Brough Park was a very substantial, indeed a grand building of two storeys - a copy of the Archbishop's Chapel at York - with a presbytery attached and associated outbuildings. The ground floor had originally been a school and the entire complex, besides being much larger than SS. Mary and Everilda, was situated on its own in a rather bleak location about a quarter of a mile from the Hall and other buildings. It was nonetheless imposing. Pevsner described it as 'a job full of fervour' and 'the proudest Catholic church in the county'.

Storey's additional responsibility in his new post was to be Chaplain to the R.A.F. Regiment at nearby Catterick where duties scarcely stretched him. Both there, and later at Bedale, he disliked one feature of military chaplaincy: as Chaplain he was regarded as an officer, which restricted opportunities for mingling with the men. Moreover, by the late 1970s the congregation at St. Paulinus was tiny and the buildings were in poor condition: visitors could not help noticing that water ran freely down at least one of the walls in the presbytery. Although fellow clergy and the monks at Ampleforth were very kind to him, Storey found the presbytery an 'unbelievable dwelling': he got no respite from going out because of the thought of what he had to come back to. Over lunch at a local hotel he had 'a long, rather hard exchange, but without bitterness' with Peter, who was himself upset by the furore caused by the change. Both men were anxious to move on from the situation and by December 1979 Storey was installed in a house the diocese acquired for him in the garrison at Catterick. Hoping for an early change of appointment, he requested and obtained 'a full head-on session' with the new bishop, Harris, who, having formerly been Auxiliary Bishop in Liverpool, was very experienced. After this, which took place in the New Year, Storey was noticeably more relaxed and up-beat. The move came in the summer: a few miles south down the A1 to the parish of SS. Mary and Joseph in Bedale. At Brough Park he had done little more than keep an unsatisfactory situation ticking over which, though he had little choice, was not his usual manner of discharging responsibilities.

He found his new situation much more congenial. He kept bees in the garden of the presbytery adjacent to the church and, again on his own as parish priest, found rather more to occupy him. In addition to his duties at the main church, he provided services at St. Columba's in Masham and at St. Theresa's in Hunton; and he was also Chaplain to the geriatric hospital at Mowbray Grange; and, less congenially, to R.A.F. Leeming.

As at Brough Park, local Catholic gentry families had played a key role in establishing and sustaining the Catholic community in and around Bedale. There was a Mass Centre there from 1771 which for a time also served Northallerton, and was followed by a church from 1812; later, financed by the Scrope family, a new church was built in 1878. It was then that Bedale became a parish in its own right. SS. Mary and Joseph is 'a good example of a small mid-Victorian Catholic church'. It was designed by the York-born architect, George Goldie, who was commissioned extensively by the diocese of Middlesbrough. In the light of the liturgical changes of Vatican II, Storey's immediate and lasting contribution was to re-order the sanctuary, with the altar being brought forward so that the celebrant faced the congregation. He also made the entrance to the church disabled-friendly. One of his parishioners was the recipient of a characteristic act of charity. One day Storey found her much distressed in the church: instead of regularly settling bills with money given to him by his mother, her son had been buying drugs, and she could see no way of discharging their debts. Storey paid them off immediately.

After only a year, he moved on yet again, this time to become Parish Priest of Holy Cross in Cottingham, just outside Hull. Although he worried about leaving his parishioners in Bedale so quickly, there was, he felt, too little to do there for someone of his energy. He was looking for a bigger challenge, one that would truly stretch him. Against the background of his recent encouraging engagement with his bishop, and learning that Fr. Philip Purcell, the current incumbent in Cottingham, was approaching retirement, he submitted an application for the post to the diocese, and was appointed. After seven years at St. Charles in Hull and a decade as University Chaplain, Cottingham was an area he knew very well indeed and he already had many friends and acquaintances in the village. Then 62 years old, he was to remain in Cottingham for fifteen years, by far his longest period in any post, and one which proved to be the most productive and rewarding of his priestly life.

CHAPTER NINE

COTTINGHAM 1981-96

Cottingham, believed by some to be the largest village in England, is long-established, with a fine medieval parish church, St. Mary's. Its growth accelerated once the railway arrived and, at just over three miles from the centre of Hull, its location was much prized by the city's wealthier merchants during the later 19th century. Some of their large houses were later converted into University halls of residence and, while Storey was Chaplain and later, much of the University's student accommodation was situated there. The church at Holy Cross was opened in 1929. Fifty years on, just before Storey's appointment, it was estimated that, along with students, there were 600 or so Catholics resident in the village and its environs.

By 1981 Monsignor Philip Purcell had been Parish Priest for a quarter of a century. Latterly he had served as a Vicar General: conscientious by nature and conservative in outlook, he was a reserved and very private person; an Irishman who had perhaps never felt comfortable in England. Under him Holy Cross saw little change and was ripe for development; and having been becalmed at Brough Park and Bedale, Storey relished the challenge.

Congregations at Holy Cross were large enough to require three Masses at weekends, a Vigil Mass on Saturday evening and two on Sunday morning. Storey's responsibilities included chaplaincies at Castle Hill hospital (full-time) and De La Pole hospital (part-time); he also visited various retirement homes in and around the village. His overriding task was to resurrect the parish - to generate vitality in all aspects of its life. Knowing the situation from earlier years, he had a clear idea of what he wanted to do and quickly moved into gear. By the end of his first year key features of his parish work were evident: plans for changes to the church building, close relations with other denominations, and fundraising for third-world projects.

The church was narrow in relation to its length and unsympathetic to the new liturgy; there was nowhere else on site where parishioners had been able to hold meetings because Monsignor Purcell had reserved the presbytery for himself; and some of the fabric of both church and presbytery needed repair and refurbishment. So, besides enlivening the parish, Storey had a complex physical task ahead of him which took some years to complete.

To minimise potential difficulties, he made sure that his parishioners travelled with him. He established a Parish Council of nine – three officers (Chairman, Treasurer and Secretary) and six other members besides himself - whose constitution provided for elections to short, three-year terms of office, with initial turnover being staggered; and as at Stokesley, nominations were made either by those wishing to stand or by others recommending them. The Council first met in February 1983. There was a regular turnover of membership and thereby a growing number gained experience of parish business.

Operations were not immediately smooth. To start with the parish did not have a gestetner, let alone a photocopier, but within a couple of years meetings took place bi-monthly on average, and agendas and minutes were circulated promptly. Financial matters were dealt with transparently and, briefed by accounts published well in advance, parishioners discussed them at an open Annual General Meeting. Normal arrangements sometimes broke down. For the AGM in March 1987 neither the agenda nor the minutes of the previous meeting were distributed, to which Storey's candid, public reaction was that the Council 'was not working as well as it should be'; and there was occasional difficulty in filling the vice-chairmanship. Nonetheless, progress overall was steady and impressive. Activities multiplied, recurrent income rose much faster than recurrent expenditure, and by 1986 it was estimated that over 1,000 people attended the parish, with 100 actively involved in running it, a marked increase on earlier years. By 1988 Storey was very satisfied: 30 names had been suggested for membership of the Parish Council, 24 of them being willing to stand. 'Whereas in the past', he announced, 'the election result had tended to be predictable, it no longer was at all'. Administrative changes were for a purpose and he regularly reminded parishioners where priorities lay.

> While we may not have any shattering impact on the great wide world, we will not do amiss if we grow as a body of folk who care and share and rejoice in the life-giving grace and company of the Lord....Up with your hearts. Spring is in the air, as the grasshopper said. To which the slug replied 'Spring in the air yourself'. Be a Grasshopper!

Major reasons for optimism were the speed and success of the building and refurbishment programmes.

Soon after arriving Storey expanded facilities near the Church entrance, making it wheelchair-friendly, and providing a kitchen and toilets and additional noticeboards. These were soon followed by developments on the north side, where the wall was removed to create a large rectangular space. Once this had been walled in, with a shallower ceiling than the rest of the church and a sliding partition at the join, re-ordering was possible. The altar and tabernacle were relocated on the opposite, south wall, fronting a much wider space than previously and with benches and seats on three sides. Most of this was completed by 1984, including windows to the rear of the new altar, repairs to the church roof and extensive re-decoration. Capital expenditure totalled £75,000, most of it financed by a bank loan which came within £3,000 of the diocese's permitted maximum. However, growth in the number of profitable functions; in covenanting, which Storey introduced and which began to 'take off' in 1985-86; and prudent management – in the two years 1985-87 £1,764 was raised from letting rooms in the presbytery to students – enabled the parish to become debt-free by the end of the decade. Refurbishment of the presbytery then proceeded with a new roof and new windows. Not everything proceeded to plan: indeed, there was a change of contractor early in the building process. Yet at the AGM in March 1985 the Chairman of the Parish Council congratulated Storey: 'the gamble of the money spent on the extension had paid off, since it was now a focal point for many…. nearly everyone was involved in parish activities….and the parish had formed itself into an alliance'.

Not everyone welcomed radical new departures. By January 1984 arrangements following the church extension 'met with majority support', but there was no unanimity. One parishioner of long standing was full of praise for much of what had occurred and welcomed the rumour that the *baldequino* - in his opinion 'a temporary ecclesiastical furnishing fad' – was also to be removed. However, he abhorred the relocation of the altar and tabernacle.

> One has a rectangular church which is being treated as though it were semi-circular: to the ordinary parishioner it is neither one thing nor the other. I know of only one parishioner who approves the new alterations: there may, of course be a few more.

In the course of four letters to the Council, another parishioner

27: The re-ordered church of Holy Cross, Cottingham.

was vituperative. When Storey refused to hold a referendum on the altar's location, he maintained that this made 'the Parish Council look like a mere fatigue-party': the Parish Priest wished 'to divide and disrupt (a well-known Communist ploy)'. Holy Cross was 'a Church and not a Concert Hall'. Successive Chairmen of the Parish Council rebutted these charges, pointing out that the Council was unanimous, and that 'other parishioners have also voiced their opinions, and the majority of these have been favourable to the new arrangement'.

While physical developments were dramatic, evoking some mixed feelings, constitutional changes were influential. Before Storey's time groups came together only when organising specific functions such as the Autumn Fayre. Meetings of the Parish Council covered everything, with sub-groups and individuals reporting to it. As matters progressed multi-tasking became common with valuable cross-fertilisation of ideas and skills. Meetings took place either in the Priory Room (the name chosen by the Council for the extension) or in the presbytery where Storey established an office, steadily improving its equipment. A magazine appeared, at first three times a year: it faltered occasionally owing to personnel problems, but persisted; and each weekend, whether or not Storey was in residence, there was a parish bulletin. Within a relatively short period his was a thoroughly fresh regime.

What transpired was akin to a series of concentric circles. Innermost was activity within the parish, which expanded continuously. From the start, however, this was set within an interdenominational context in the village and its vicinity. For Storey it was axiomatic that a commitment to ecumenism involved regular, joint activity with all other Christian groups. A third circle encompassed the city of Hull and the diocese as a whole. Meetings and events were listed in the bulletin and transport was arranged/shared wherever possible. Finally, through extensive fundraising, much of it via CAFOD, Holy Cross became linked with many places overseas, most notably through its twinning with a parish in Sierra Leone. Storey was determined that Holy Cross do its utmost to alleviate poverty and misfortune at home and abroad. Through endeavours in these four spheres the parish was steadily transformed.

There were significant developments in the parish's worship and liturgy, many emanating (via the diocese) from Vatican II, all espoused enthusiastically by Storey, and the majority designed to boost lay participation - bidding prayers, Eucharistic ministers, penitential services, Communion under both kinds, and - this time successfully – female as well as male altar servers. The Parish Council became involved in organising Holy

28: Storey conducting a baptism at Holy Cross.

Week services, when a visiting priest led a retreat or delivered a series of talks. Choristers such as the Ampleforth Singers occasionally sang at Sunday Masses. With spouses particularly (though not solely) in mind, special Masses were held for non-Catholics: parishioners were encouraged to invite them and guests were urged *not* to contribute to collections. All proceedings in church were enhanced by a new PA system. In addition to establishing a prayer group, the parish participated in diocesan consultations, producing no fewer than four house groups involved in preparations for the international Synod on 'The Laity and the Church' in 1987; and at the request of the bishop, following this up with further house meetings on 'Morality Today'.

Other activities were diverse. Annually they included not just a very busy Catholic Women's League programme and a traditional Autumn Fayre, but also a Spring Dance; a parish outing, for example to a theme park, the Saxon crypt at Ripon Minster or the York Mystery Plays; a treasure hunt around Cottingham; a parish dinner at a local restaurant or in the University; and a summer barbecue at a parishioner's farm. Parishioners held garden parties at their homes (with Storey sometimes selling honey from his hives at the presbytery). There was a Harvest Festival followed by a Concert, whose proceeds were customarily donated to the Friends of Castle Hill hospital. There were visits to the theatre, outings for the altar servers, and parish rambles through the countryside. At Christmas the youngest parishioners were invited to help to decorate the church and assemble the crib, and donations to the crib-box were given to HARP, a charity for the 'homeless and rootless'. There were parties at New Year for the elderly, housebound and disabled and a parish branch of the St. Vincent de Paul Society kept an eye on the poor and lonely. Since there was no Catholic school in the parish Storey and other parishioners provided catechesis – involving three or four separate age-groups – for children attending state schools; and until the local authority footed the bill (from 1988-89), a parish 200 Club subsidised transport for pupils attending Catholic schools in the Hull area. Storey was particularly alive to opportunities for teenagers. Despite faltering periodically, as when four of its leading lights left simultaneously for university, a parish Youth Club flourished for several years. When it folded, its age-group was pointed in the direction of 'Springboard' events at Ampleforth and meetings of CAYA (the Catholic Association of Young Adults). While most of these developments were prompted by Storey, some were initiated by parishioners: a mother and toddler group, a bowls team of which Storey was a regular member and which played in the local Catholic league, and a Holy Cross fantasy football fundraising scheme which quickly enlisted 27 teams. By the mid-1980s the atmosphere in the parish was vibrant, and remained so.

Ecumenical endeavour went far beyond the routinely conventional. Holy Cross became an active member of the local Council of Churches whose meetings, in turn with other locations, were held in the Priory Room. The Council organised a lively programme for church unity week, including a joint Barn Dance; produced leaflets giving details of members' services at Christmas and Easter, together with an invitation and a poster, which the laity delivered door-to-door throughout the village; and designed and delivered joint lecture series, some as part of church programmes and others at the local College of Further Education. They regularly combined to raise money for Christian Aid and other charities, such as the Salvation Army's Social Fund. Each Good Friday they walked through Cottingham carrying a large cross; and they jointly ran the programme 'Mission England' and several local 'Songs of Praise' in the village. They participated in joint study groups in Lent, with members of various denominations outlining the basis of their faith. Some of these activities went on elsewhere in the Hull area, but in variety and extent Cottingham had no competitors. At one point Storey invited young female parishioners at Holy Cross to join the Girls' Brigade if they so wished, and towards the end of his time as parish priest he began to include meetings in local synagogues (of the local Council of Christians and Jews, for example) among notices in the bulletin.

There was much collaboration between local parishes in north Humberside, especially in raising money for charity. Holy Cross also joined others in petitioning against the opening of sex shops in the city, in favour of parents being consulted by general practitioners about prescriptions for under-16-year-olds, and in lobbying Parliament for sanctions against South Africa. Storey's personal contribution to one development was seminal, viz. the re-establishment of an Amnesty International group in the area. He had been a member of the national organisation since 1962, the year after its formation. However, the Hull branch had been wound up in the early 1980s. It took some time to resurrect it, though from his arrival at Holy Cross Storey got a small band of parishioners, meeting at first in their homes, involved in writing to heads of state and senior officials in support of prisoners of conscience. He became closely engaged in fundraising for Amnesty, beginning with a concert at Hull Guildhall in June 1982. Either there or at the Ferens Art Gallery in the city, this subsequently became an annual event, held in the early New Year. By the autumn of 1986 matters had progressed sufficiently for a new group for the Hull region to be inaugurated. It flourished, meeting monthly, often in the Priory Room. Their first 'adopted' prisoner, Albert, a Jehovah's Witness who had been gaoled in the USSR for objecting to military service, was freed after two years. Having sent 800 cards to prisoners in December 1990, the group set a target of 1,000 for the following year, and there was loud rejoicing when another of 'their' prisoners, a Dr. U. Tin Myo Win, was set free in Burma in June 1990. Later, ten members of Syria's Committee for Democratic Freedoms, imprisoned by President Assad, were freed following support from the Hull Amnesty group.

Amnesty complemented another sphere of activity, international in scope, raising awareness of the plight of third-world countries and forging links with them. On arrival at Holy Cross Storey's deep interest in poverty and underdevelopment was firmly established. He felt unable to continue as Chairman of the diocesan Commission of Justice and Peace but was always an active member. In Cottingham the parish became involved in CAFOD's family fast day scheme whereby households went without one meal per week, and donated the money saved to different projects each year: for Polish children's charities in 1982, local medical centres in Peru in 1983, water schemes in Sierra Leone in 1984, and so on. Simultaneously, the parish contributed to Mother Theresa's charities and the Ethiopian famine appeal. Once the church extension was underway a Traidcraft stall was established, selling tea and coffee, and later dried fruits, spices and other items – all this while discharging the parish's building debt at a healthy rate. While weekly collections at Mass averaged around £250 in the early 1980s and were approaching £500 by the mid-1990s (partly because of congregational growth under Storey), large funds were separately raised for various international projects. Targets were set in the parish and before long Holy Cross regularly met or exceeded them.

Yet, while fundraising was impressive, by September 1985 Storey found the lack of support in other respects 'very depressing'. People did not want to understand third-world problems, he thought, because 'they merely engendered feelings of gloom and powerlessness'. A month later he felt that earlier efforts to establish a third-world group 'had fizzled out'. In fact the seeds of future success were already sown.

Local history was helpful. William Wilberforce (1759-1833), the leading advocate of the abolition of slavery, was a native of Hull: he was M.P. for the city from 1780 and later represented Yorkshire at Westminster. Among his endeavours was the foundation of a homeland, Sierra Leone in West Africa, for freed slaves. From 1792 growing numbers of them went there from North America. Sierra Leone became a British colony in 1808 and from 1961 an independent republic within the Commonwealth. In 1979 Hull and Freetown, the capital of Sierra Leone, established a civic partnership and, a year later, an official twinning arrangement; and in 1981 a Freetown Society was formed in Hull. P. J. (Paddy) Doyle, the leader of Hull City Council, was particularly active in promoting the Society and also fostered other links with Sierra Leone. At the parish AGM in March 1985 Storey announced that Mr. Doyle had recommended that Holy Cross adopt a Catholic parish in Freetown – St. Anthony's in the suburb of Wilberforce – with the objective of rebuilding the school there at an estimated cost of £5,000. In May Storey undertook to raise £2,000 of this and to petition CAFOD for the rest. It was during that summer that he shared with parishioners his fear of failure in regard to third-world issues, and this seems to have galvanised them. By February 1986 £2,000 had already been sent to West Africa. There was a brief pause while the parish joined others during Lent in raising money for a project in Chile, but by year-end the rebuilding of St. Anthony's school was finished, with Holy Cross having contributed £4,000.

As Holy Cross's debts were reduced, the parish was generous to others too, and in 1987-88 sent £1,000 to a project in Bangladesh, £1,500 to another in Mozambique, and £1,000 to a third in Ethiopia; and by November 1988 had met its target of £1,000 for workshops for the disabled in Peru. In January 1989 it sent £1,000 towards a scheme in Kampuchea, and went on to join Hull parishes in raising money for a refuge being established in Recife, Brazil, by its archbishop, Dom Helder Camara. A commitment to Sierra Leone had, however, taken root. Holy Cross gave £230 to a single retiring collection for 'the poor of Freetown' in April 1989, Paddy Doyle addressed a parish meeting in May, and in November there arrived photographs of the school at St. Anthony's. In 1990 Holy Cross agreed to raise money to furnish and equip the school. Such help soon became vital because between 1991 and 2002 Sierra Leone was plunged into a vicious civil war. Tens of thousands of people were killed, maimed and/or displaced, there was massive destruction of infrastructure, and public life was profoundly disrupted.

In May 1991, against this background, Holy Cross made what according to Storey was its 'highest [one-off] contribution' to a third-world emergency - £1,300 to the 'African Disaster

Fund' – and the city-wide Lent project for 1992 was for a clinic, school, water supply and waste disposal unit for Wilberforce village. Then, Holy Cross's extraordinary efforts for Sierra Leone having clearly been recognised, there was a massive change of gear. Fr. Bert Veal, Parish Priest of St, Mary's, Chelsea, who had been visiting Wilberforce, came to Cottingham to discuss the possibility of the parish being twinned, not with St. Anthony's, but with a parish, Our Lady Star of the Sea, to be newly established at Juba on the coast on the outskirts of Freetown. The formal invitation to twin was delivered by Archbishop Ganda of Freetown during a visit to Holy Cross at the beginning of June. The proceeds of that year's Autumn Fayre were devoted to the project, and 'topped £1,500'. In December a Committee of seven was established to oversee the twinning, and in February 1993 (the Golden Jubilee of Storey's ordination) two parishioners, one a doctor, travelled to Juba to assess local needs, taking with them an initial gift of £2,000.

The parish continued to help other parts of the world as well as other projects in Sierra Leone: by the end of May 1993, for instance, Holy Cross had donated £1,000 to the funds being raised by all the Catholic parishes in Hull to finance a new hospital in Freetown. The twinning, however, got top priority. Among its benefits were the solidity and longevity which it brought to relations between Cottingham and Juba, whose needs became subject to systematic enquiry and analysis. There was considerable scope for accumulating gifts in kind as well as money, thereby involving more people more directly in the effort. Especially in wartime, logistics benefited from advice and experience as contacts on both sides grew in number and variety. Fundraising efforts diversified and came to include more events in parishioners' own homes and a growing variety of sponsored activities. Gifts in kind were mobilised on a quasi-industrial scale. By the end of 1993 36 tea-chests, containing typewriters, sewing machines, tools, books, toys and many other items, had been despatched, together each quarter with a carton of medical supplies. A priest, Fr. Sylvester Wuya, was appointed to the new parish in July 1993 and, though not quite completed, the church of Our Lady Star of the Sea was officially opened in October. Storey and three of his parishioners from Holy Cross (two of whom were students engaged in third-world studies) were guests and brought with them £2,000 worth of vestments, chalices, missals and memorial cards. Their travels around the area included a visit to a refugee camp holding 45,000 people, many of them victims of linked troubles in nearby Liberia. By July 1994 the number of tea-chests despatched from Cottingham had risen to 70. Despite the war, there was regular contact between the twins, including a visit to Cottingham by Dr. Kanu, Chairman of the Parish Council of Our Lady Star of the Sea, who showed a video of the church's opening. Storey and his colleagues strove to identify what they might most usefully do, and their African friends sent detailed advice as to how money and goods could be transmitted most securely. A major gift from Holy Cross was a generator which helped St. Mary's to cope with recurrent power cuts during the civil war.

Storey's efforts were sustained beyond his time and by the early years of the new millennium Our Lady's had within its compound the church, a house, a nursery, the Stella Maris Primary School, a bakery, a clinic, a vocational centre staffed by volunteers, and a multi-purpose hall, all built with assistance from Holy Cross. The parish also supported an orphanage in Bo, Sierra Leone's second city, while continuing to finance development at Stella Maris School, providing new classrooms, furniture and materials, and subsidising many pupils. A decade or so after the end of the civil war Sierra Leone suffered a devastating outbreak of Ebola, and there was a landslide disaster in 2017, with relief coming from Cottingham for both. So relations between Holy Cross and St. Mary's, Juba have continued in what has been the most enduring of Storey's legacies.

The scale of Holy Cross's generosity was very substantial indeed. It was a relatively wealthy parish with more than the average quota of professional, middle-class commuters. In seeking to generate commitment among his parishioners Storey was also helped by the regional context. The policies of the Labour-controlled Hull City Council towards Sierra Leone were influential and the Justice and Peace Commission, originally inspired by Storey himself of course, provided a strong diocesan context. First among additional factors was Storey's boundless energy. One example should suffice. On 20 February 1994 he inserted the following notice in the parish bulletin.

> A.J.S. aet. 75 plus 1/365, proposes to walk 21 miles (North Dalton – Wetwang – Huggate – Fridaythorpe), and proposes you should sponsor him to create transport pennies for our Freetown tea-chests. Forms available next week.

A month later, he and some companions having gathered £835 in sponsorship, he told his parishioners: 'You're a fabulous lot – that's 4 times 9 tea-chests….How soon can you bear an encore?' The sum total collected eventually came to £1,278. Most people his age would never have contemplated the challenge.

Secondly, his parishioners came to realise that prioritisation of the poor and unfortunate – whether they lived in some far-flung part or just down the road – was the dominant feature of his approach to pastoral life. As in Middlesbrough years before, it ran through everything he did; and, like the post-war inhabitants of the Grove Hill estate, it won him huge respect and strong support. Alongside his eye-catching endeavours for the third world, there were persistent, if more mundane, efforts at home. At one point he stated simply that 'I am always pleased to hear of any furniture, carpets etc. which could be of use to some family. Please remember this'. He solicited an 'electric cooker for one poor person' and a 'small working fridge' for another. He sought jobs for the poor and unemployed: 'a young man seeks work on a Saturday, for a few hours'; 'a young man wants a day's garden work'. In the early years, before it was regularly devoted to hospital funds, the proceeds of the sale of produce after the Harvest Festival was 'for the poor'. The contents of the St. Vincent de Paul box were earmarked 'for poor folk'. The small garden at the presbytery had a holly tree which, each year, produced copious red berries. Storey cut down laden branches, left them on the lawn, and invited parishioners to take them and leave a donation either for CAFOD or 'the poor'. Among his more frequent requests was for accommodation – for students and would-be au pairs, but also for foster parents for young people and for families in need. Various moneys were set aside for a Lourdes fund. It was parish policy 'to allow one sick person to go, without cost, each year'. Perhaps his most unusual intervention came just before Christmas 1987 when there was a scare about British nationality. 'If any of you do not have it and wish to apply, you should do so before December 31st. If you do not know how to, contact me at once'. Involved discreetly in prison work himself, he encouraged others to join the Board of Visitors at Hull Prison: it was 'important work'. His duties at Castle Hill hospital involved regular visits at normal times, but also urgent calls at all hours of the day and night. He earned the great respect of the staff there for the way he dealt with patients, notably their first AIDS victim. He not only fundraised for the hospital but kept parishioners informed of special needs with which they might volunteer help, either with aspects of the service or with individual patients. He was responsive to need wherever it arose.

Storey and many others suspected that he would flourish in Cottingham. The only time that his spirits flagged was when he felt, mistakenly, that his efforts on the third-world front had failed. He worked extremely hard and virtually everything he did was infected with *joie de vivre*. He made the following announcement in February 1985:

> Shrove Tuesday 3.00 p,m. All, children, youth, wrinklies and crumblies under the age of 85 invited to the International Carrington Pancake Races. Refreshments and ritual munching of bruised pancakes afterwards.

The event was not repeated. Perhaps it caused too much commotion in quiet, suburban Carrington Avenue, though the service in the church on Shrove Tuesday 1996 was followed by the consumption of almost 200 pancakes. He was happy to turn humour on himself, listing a talk he gave later in 1985 as 'Why Get Married? A Scriptural Survey by Rev. A.J. Storey (who didn't)'; and on 3 January 1988 a 'Party for old folk, i.e. everyone older than me'. In the following June:

> Big Red Bins of books for kiddiwinks to distract them from super sermons lie at the door of the Priory Room at each Mass, for them to take, and PUT BACK, after the jaw is over.

His congregations would have been intrigued by the following message in 1990, 'I am looking for a translation from Turkish. Any offers?' He had received a reply to an Amnesty letter from a Turkish prisoner: a visit to a Turkish restaurant in Hull solved the problem. Another notice a year later dealt with more mundane business: 'Autumn manoeuvres in your garden. If you are removing redundant shrubs, please let me know – I could use them'. He was punctilious in telling everyone about forthcoming absences and in August 1987 explained one unavoidable alteration in supply arrangements for his holiday in Crete:

> I do not think it right to leave you so long without a priest,
> but it has happened suddenly and it reminds us that you, the
> church community, must grow in your own prayer, and
> scripture reading, and the Eucharist, with priests being less
> numerous (or in Crete).

And when both he and his curate were absent from 4 - 8 July
1994: 'Retreat for all the clergy of the diocese at Ampleforth. Try
not to die, and delay all else, during those days'. He was
remarkably phlegmatic even when some of his best-laid plans
were thwarted by a poor response. Having established a parish
lending library, he had to complain about books being taken and
not returned, but only in the following terms: 'Bad! No Brownie
Points.... Penalty – Banishment, i.e. excommunication'.
Noticeably, in contrast to his changeable moods earlier in his
career, in Cottingham he was nearly always sunny-side-up.
'Some kind person left a CD player in the presbytery weeks ago!
I would like to know who it was and, if it was a gift, to say
whoopee! and *thank-you!*'. He was at ease with his parishioners,
and they with him

Although Storey was aways remarkably fit for his age, it
was taxing in his 60s and 70s to create the infrastructure to
sustain, and then to preside over, this wide range of parish
activity. He found time, however, for other things. Rearing trees
was his favourite pastime. This began long before he arrived at
Holy Cross, but he invited parishioners there to join him, using
the small presbytery garden to raise saplings of oak, beech and
hazel, and then transplanting them elsewhere. When visiting
anyone he would invariably walk round their garden, offering
advice, especially about trees, and made innumerable plantings.
Especially during this period when he was helped by

parishioners, he established several thousand trees to the north of the lane leading to the Lady Chapel at Mount Grace. Other sites included one at Melbourne near Market Weighton, where he was joined on one occasion by over a dozen parishioners; a parishioner's farm at Leven, on the way to Hornsea; and the grounds of both Castle Hill hospital in Cottingham and St. Mary's College in north Hull. Undoubtedly there were other sites. He was a lively member of the R.S.P.B. and the Woodland Trust and once took a group from Holy Cross to Glen Affric in the Scottish Highlands where they worked for 'Trees for Life'. Trees were not just a major interest: they were a consuming passion, and birds were not far behind.

According to one contemporary, the expansion of Storey's congregations at Holy Cross was 'due in no small measure to his spiritual intensity and the remarkable variety and richness of his eloquent sermons'. His reputation as a preacher spread steadily and before long he was much in demand as a broadcaster and writer too. He was regularly commissioned by Radio Humberside for 'Just a Thought' and 'Thought for the Day', by Yorkshire Television for 'Epilogue' and 'Five Minutes', and by East Yorkshire newspapers for 'Thought for the Week' and other articles. Busy though he was, he valued these opportunities to reach wider audiences.

His single most prestigious commission was for a sermon before a packed congregation in York Minster on 7 October 1990 - the first there by a Catholic priest since the Reformation – when he addressed the senior judiciary at the annual dedication service of the North Eastern Circuit. He began with Christ's words to Pilate: 'You would have no power over me if it had not been given to you from above', and then stated unequivocally that at a dedication service 'your Oath, and Covenant and Consecration is….to the true, the just, the right and the fair'. He went on to maintain that, although society was pluralist, there was no-one among them without belief, because of values which were the objects of belief. Values were not created, they were found; and the balance to be struck in identifying them was between the common good and the rightful freedom of the individual. Christianity demanded that each individual be regarded as sacrosanct. Special regard for the weak was not an optional extra: it was central to their calling, just as it was to his as a priest. Moreover, in justly sentencing they must always have an eye to the restoration of the individuals involved; and police, prison governors and all in authority over those sentenced must keep this at the forefront of their minds.

> And there is one area where the weight and power of you all should be unremitting – there are…. persons, who attempt and commit suicide in no small numbers in our disgraceful jails, sometimes while still on remand. Against that we must cry out….A priest friend of mine was committed briefly to prison for refusing to pay a fine for daubing the Ministry of Defence one Ash Wednesday: no slopping out for him.

Storey knew what he was talking about, having worked quietly with prisoners for years, for Amnesty International, and 'rarely' missing a meeting of the Justice and Peace Commission. The congregation heard nothing anodyne that day before trooping off to their customary banquet in the Merchant Adventurers' Hall.

Having taught on a very part-time basis at St. Mary's School, in 1988 Storey was appointed Sixth-Form Chaplain at the newly-instituted St. Mary's College. The College was a major outcome of the educational restructuring of the 1980s instigated by Bishop Harris. It was important that the new institution flourished and the bishop undoubtedly had this in mind in appointing assistants for Storey at Holy Cross, who took up the space in the presbytery previously occupied by students. Fr. John Wood came as Curate for the two years from 1987 and was followed for five years by Fr. Roy Lovatt. Originally a Methodist and later the Anglican Rector of St. Paul's in Hull, the latter was married with children, so Holy Cross was among the first Catholic parishes to be served by a married priest. Similar to arrangements made by Fr. Knowles in Hull years earlier, parish priest and curate divided home visiting between them geographically, with Storey taking west Cottingham and Fr Lovatt the east. Finally, John Bane joined Storey from Ushaw College from September until December 1995, in advance of his ordination in July 1997. When he took up his duties at St. Mary's Storey had help from these colleagues and the active support of many laity, and so was able to pursue matters which had been beyond him during his early years at Holy Cross.

St. Mary's College had a team of chaplains, each one attached to a particular age-group. He led an assembly each Tuesday morning and said Mass on special occasions – at the beginning of term, on holy days, before Christmas and Easter, and just before students finally left the College. Occasionally there were whole-school Masses when the chaplains concelebrated and he was on the rota for the daily Masses in the College Chapel. Two annual priorities were the day of recollection arranged for each group off-site, in which the chaplain played a major role; and the Sixth-Form Formal. According to one teacher, 'his assemblies and services were legendary'. He particularly relished helping out in religious education classes for any group, but especially for the sixth form, with whom there were lively discussions of philosophical and ethical issues.

In 1993-94 he was involved with College staff in designing a Health and Sex Education Policy. He was unequivocal about this: 'calling the Art of Loving a Health and Sex Education Policy seems to me very questionable indeed'. Nonetheless, he became fully engaged, revealing how his views, on a subject which he had always regarded as critically important, had developed. It was crucial, he believed, to recognise a fundamental difference between animals and human beings. For the former, sexual activity was governed by the hormonal readiness of the female to receive the male, and was entirely geared towards offspring; for the latter, male and female could unite sexually without any thought of it being fruitful. And because the attraction of one for the other was there from puberty onwards, there had to be 'a very strong discipline of the virtue of chastity'. For in the Divine Plan, he believed, 'the giving of one's whole self to another....is not meant to be used outside a relationship of committed permanence'. Moreover (echoing an article which he had had published in *Priests and People* in September 1987, 'Marriage in Holy Writ'), in the New Testament:

> nowhere....is marriage spoken of as having for its purpose procreation. St. Paul speaks of the relationship entirely in terms of the imaging of God's kind of loving - namely total, unto death, for the building of each other into the image of God.

It followed, therefore, that the discovery of secure methods of birth control was 'something positively wonderful': women no longer had to be burdened with numerous children, and husband and wife were able 'to rejoice in their unity'. Full knowledge of birth control methods should never, he went on, be withheld from young people.

> To deny them that knowledge and expect that they are going to go through their adolescence without sexual expression is simply unrealistic....[But] as a teacher, I feel I can make it quite clear that it is always morally wrong to make love outside commitment.

Teaching must be 'firm', but 'recognition of the situation must be real'.

In remembering him people did not of course focus on his views on particular matters. Hundreds, perhaps thousands, of people retain clear memories of the man, and what they recall most vividly is the private impact Storey had on their lives - his personal touches, which were often indelible. One maintained that Storey:

> plucked me out of my life stream when I asked him if I could put a few Christmas lights on the conifer tree at the entrance to [Holy Cross]....When later I was in a work recession he again raised me up to re-wire the priest's house....His mandate, he always said, was to disturb the comfortable and....comfort the disturbed.

Another parishioner was a trades union official. Stressed by having to deal with redundancies, he visited church one morning to pray before going to work. He was no sooner there than Storey was kneeling beside him, knowing of his trouble and having looked out for him. During another difficult period Storey told him: 'you are a long blade of grass, you will bend in the wind, but you will not break'. One pair of his female altar servers felt that:

> We were possibly the worst altar servers in the history of the church. Every other Sunday without fail for over two years we put the candles in the wrong place, rang bells at the wrong time and stood helplessly at the side of the altar hoping the priest would tell us what to pass him at that particular point....Through the whole debacle Fr. Tony never showed any sign of losing his patience or his sense of humour. He would just quietly and gently tell us....what we were supposed to be doing next.

Many marvelled at his knowledge and experience of rural life. 'He almost went into a world of his own, so at home did he seem in the countryside'. Walking along a forest path during one parish ramble, he suddenly stooped down and picked up a dormouse. 'He said it wouldn't live long unless he removed a tic'; and having done so and put the mouse under some bracken, he moved on. A daughter of one parishioner suffered so severely from anorexia that she was hospitalized in Hull. She did not speak to visitors who, therefore, did not return. Storey visited her regularly, making no attempt to speak but simply sharing her silence. They then corresponded and she made a full recovery, qualifying as a mental health nurse and earning a fine reputation.

Such reminiscences are legion and help to explain the love felt for Storey by his parishioners. During his 15 years in Cottingham there were three occasions in particular when they were able, collectively, to show what they felt about him. The first was in February 1983, not long after his arrival - the Ruby Jubilee of his ordination. There are no details of precisely what occurred, except for his remarks in the Bulletin for 20 February.

> Thank you so much. Quite overwhelming, for which overwhelmment [sic] I do apologise. But I do thank you all most sincerely. You have and will go on having my prayer for you at every Mass.

A decade later, on Sunday 14 February 1993, Storey reached his Golden Jubilee. The Parish Council ensured that this was celebrated in some style, inviting every parishioner. Bishop John Crowley and his Auxiliary, Bishop Kevin O'Brien, both attended, concelebrating with Storey at the 10.30 Mass. In his homily that day Storey reflected on major changes following his ordination, the first of which was later to be the subject of one of his last publications.

> Since then the Church's understanding of priesthood has undergone a revolution: that change has been central to my experience. Scarcely less momentous has been the

*29: Sunday 14 February 1993. Storey celebrating the Golden
Jubilee of his Ordination, flanked (left) by Bishop John
Crowley and (right) by the Auxiliary Bishop, Kevin O'Brien.*

developing understanding of womanhood; and other
changes have struck me as deeply worthy of comment - the
separation and distancing of Church from State as a matter
of principle, and the proclamation of freedom of religion.

After the service everyone went to the Civic Hall in Cottingham
for a party which lasted all afternoon. The crowd included clerical
friends, representatives from parishes where Storey had
previously served, staff from St. Mary's College and the two
hospitals, and a large group from Churches Together in
Cottingham. According to Revd. David Greenwood of the Zion
United Reformed Church, 'along with so many other people in
Cottingham we have come to hold Father Tony in high esteem,
respect and love during our time here'. Storey thanked all of them
for their generous present – the cost of a return trip to Australia

to visit his brother, John (which he made in 1994), and 'for a wonderful celebration'. A month later, in *Priests and People* for April 1993, he felt able to say: 'in spite of all the tensions in the Church, and the storm-tossed world outside, I come towards the last lap with an ever deepening joy'.

Storey retired as Parish Priest at Easter 1996, shortly after his 77th birthday, and was replaced by Fr. Pat Day, an Ulsterman previously in charge of St. Stephen's Pastoral Centre in Hull. Because of the crowded nature of Holy Week and the dislocation of the subsequent holiday period, Holy Cross waited until Sunday 23 June to mark the occasion. Both bishops already had full diaries in Middlesbrough and could not attend. Bishop Crowley had 'the highest regard for Fr. Tony and all that he has done in so many ways for the diocese'. Bishop O'Brien was 'very sorry to see him going but I think it is right that he should for his own sake – he has worked very hard'. Once again, after a concelebrated Mass, the guests – some 350-400 of them – made their way to the Civic Hall. There, before a buffet lunch, Canon Michael Davern, years earlier a colleague of Storey's at Corpus Christi in Middlesbrough, presided over several presentations. The parish gave him a car (his current one had over 100,000 miles on the clock) and a word processor. There was a television set and a video recorder from the Catholic Women's League, and gifts from the Altar Servers, the Cottingham Churches and others, including a painting of St. Charles's Church in Jarratt Street, Hull, by a local artist, Monica Cook. The venue was appropriate: it was a civic as well as a parish occasion. As Revd. David Greenwood put it, 'Fr. Storey has been a tremendous friend to all of our churches, and to Cottingham'.

Among the countless tributes after Storey's death in 2007, perhaps the most revealing was from someone who, as a girl and young woman, had been among his parishioners at Holy Cross.

In very few places in my life have I seen or felt a sense of community like there was at Holy Cross. Tony was the great shining light at the heart of this, showing his love and teaching us all what the combined power of a group of like-minded individuals could achieve.

I've lost track of the number of spheres in my life that Tony influenced. His far-sighted concern for the planet we live on, caring for those less able to care for themselves and a strong sense of justice and equality for all ….He has taught me many of the important lessons in my life but, of all of them, his encouragement to stand on my own two feet, to speak up for what I believe and take responsibility for my own actions.

He led his parishioners in the way in which they should live all aspects of their lives.

CHAPTER TEN

RETIREMENT

Like others before him, Storey's feelings on retirement, apart from relief that he had made it, were apprehension and uncertainty. He was more conscious of what he was leaving behind than of what lay ahead. Sensibly, using capital left him by his parents, he had planned a break overseas. In the autumn of 1996 he greatly enjoyed 'a fine month in the Rockies, & Vancouver & the Island & [the] Pacific Rim'. On his return he was refreshed and buoyant.

> I've done it. Am free! Feel like our horses being put out to grass after the winter at home, years ago – such bucking & rearing & galloping.

The diocese had offered him accommodation in Nazareth House in Middlesbrough or at the Bar Convent in York, and was uneasy about creating a precedent through Holy Cross's wish to use the proceeds of a legacy in acquiring a house for him. In addition to their other gifts, the parish made available in Goddard Avenue, Hull, 'a nice little semi – no traffic but open land & an old railway embankment & trees & rabbits & the odd fox visiting the garden'. He had yet to get down to a planned programme but hoped:

> to get disciplined into working in the *mornings* & leaving housework & washing & shopping & garden and all that crappy world of chores until after midday. It's easy for the day to fritter by.

As always, Storey prized his independence, but in a location and among a community which he knew well.

Those living next door to him were initially apprehensive but soon came to regard Storey as 'quite simply the best neighbour we ever had'. Any waverers were won over at his first New Year in Goddard Avenue, 1997, when he organised 'nearly all of the neighbours outside onto the road to count down the old year and welcome in the new'. His instinctive generosity left an abiding impression. He kept open house to the point where it was often difficult to know who was staying with him and for how long. One neighbour, a prison officer, was startled to find a former inmate outside Storey's house waiting for him to return. If his friends in the country left vegetables and eggs, they were invariably shared with his neighbours; and after his frequently used record player suddenly disappeared, they learned eventually that he had given it to a friend whose own had broken down. In return they helped him to prune the overgrown hawthorn hedges flanking the railway embankment; to take and rear cuttings from Indian bean trees which he discovered in the neighbourhood; and, even on holiday, collected acorns for planting in his garden. He continued his tree planting until the end of his life.

Certain other activities which he regarded as key, such as meetings of the Justice and Peace Commission, also continued. He joined members at Barmoor House near Hutton-le-Hole in north Yorkshire. This was an Edwardian property built originally by Leeds Quakers, but since 1982 available for hire by religious and educational groups. They went there annually for residential meetings, often with youngsters in tow. The latter were startled by Storey's eagerness to join in any sort of game and viewed him as 'someone to aspire to, naturally a loving person with what seemed an infinite amount of knowledge', especially of trees, birds and everything else in the countryside. He said Mass either in the sitting-room or on the grass outside, and his homilies 'lit up our world'. He remained very active in the Hull Amnesty group, continuing to promote their annual concert, and also the Wilberforce Lecture, established in 1995 and devoted to human rights issues. Like others, he regretted Amnesty's shift of focus, away from personalised activism on behalf of individuals and towards fundraising for work on broader issues, but the organisation always retained his loyalty. He was also ready to help in any way at St. Mary's College and periodically said Mass and discussed matters with staff and pupils. A new Sixth-Form Centre at the College was named after him. At the Millennium, having taken cuttings from a yew tree which he reckoned was over 2,000 years old, he planted one in the College grounds, confident that it would still be there in the year 3000.

One activity in his retirement was new to Storey, although it was a natural extension of his broadcasting in the 1980s and early 1990s. With Val Goldsack and others he made three compact discs. Each one was on a different theme, combining Storey's words with appropriate songs and other music. The first, *Always With Us*, appeared in 1998. *Hear My Prayer* followed in 2001, and *Loving God* was produced during the autumn and winter of 2006-7, shortly before his death. He enjoyed this and regarded the discs as 'very important work'.

While an immensely busy parish priest Storey had managed to study and write and, with more free time at his disposal, he continued to do so. As a clerical student and newly-ordained priest, he had deplored the Church's neglect of the laity. He had warmly welcomed two of Pius XII's encyclicals, which sought to re-define their role; and was delighted by its comprehensive reformulation in *Lumen Gentium,* which he regarded as the key decree of Vatican II. His approach as a parish priest was to ensure that in terms of the layout of his churches and other arrangements the new role of the laity was able to flourish. Pope John Paul II's efforts during a long pontificate to stifle many of the results of Vatican II, particularly in this regard, greatly dismayed him. Storey's characteristic response was to carry on reading and thinking about the issue, and the eventual result was a short but vigorous article, 'Collaborative Ministry'. Citing Peter, Paul and Revelations, Storey maintained that there is only one priesthood of Christ, and that all the baptised share in it.

> The essential difference between the ordained and the lay is in their Orders, not in their Priesthood....It can be overstated, but at present tends constantly to be understated.

Each sacrament was a celebration of our priestly ministry. Correctly, the ordained minister was now named President at the Eucharist, and no longer seen as the only one in a sacrificial role. The first Eucharistic Prayer expressed the jointness of the offering with great clarity: 'We, your people and your ministers....we offer to you....' According to *Lumen Gentium,* while members of the Church in sacred orders were 'orientated chiefly and expressly to the sacred ministry', the task of the laity was to seek the kingdom in the world: but we were all equal in a universal call to priesthood. Storey saw his main task as a minister at the altar and in the pulpit 'to lead my brothers and sisters in Christ to grasp their priesthood, and to exercise it using their own initiative, not just waiting on 'Father's' permission'. Although not published until January 2007 shortly before his death, the article was completed a decade earlier in December 1997. Writing to friends at that time Storey felt that 'the issue receives little publicity because it is a clerical church still & there is no desire to know what revolution lies in Vatican II - a smouldering volcano'.

In October 1998, Storey made a candid contribution to *The Tablet's* then current discussion of the Church's refusal to allow divorced and re-married Catholics to receive Communion, prefacing his views with a tale from his days at St. Charles. A woman whose children had become Catholics sought instruction for herself and, after a few meetings, her husband asked to join her. On the eve of their reception, going through the procedure for Confession, she asked whether she needed to say that 28 years previously, aged 16, she thought she was pregnant by a boy of 17 and had married him in the local parish church. Fr. Knowles consulted the bishop who said that, as they were invalidly married, they could be received into the Church, but could not receive Communion unless they promised to live as brother and sister. They would not so promise and went their way.

The Church's position remained exactly the same said Storey, but 'need not be'.

> *Epikeia,* or equity, in regard to church law, may be invoked: that is to say, in a situation where a person's reasonable and just need falls outside the letter of the law, the person has priority. I have since invoked this principle on many occasions, and I believe it is seriously underused in many such cases. On Sabbath days, Jesus frequently invoked it. Since that occasion, I have exercised my ministry on the principle that no person who sincerely approaches the Lord needs to be trapped in a cul-de-sac.

As he matured in his pastoral role Storey refused to adopt an exclusively juridical approach. Instead, he sought to bridge the gap between conventional theological principles and mundane everyday life.

As the millennium approached he turned to something which had intrigued him for decades, the history of the Lady Chapel on the hill above the remains of Mount Grace in north Yorkshire. The ruins of the Chapel had been re-discovered by his brother, Peter, and a fellow curate immediately after the war. Both brothers, but with Peter in the lead, were involved in later developments. In the early 1950s, beset by death duties, Sir Hugh Bell, the owner of the estate where it was situated, sold

30: The Lady Chapel at Mount Grace, near Osmotherley.

the Lady Chapel to the Catholic Scrope and Eldon families, who later donated them to the diocese of Middlesbrough. Strongly encouraged by both brothers, the diocese held services there and the Chapel once more became a place of pilgrimage. Fr. Peter died in 2001, naming Storey as one of two executors. Having accumulated a good deal of historical evidence, including earlier work on the subject by a specialist on ancient shrines, H. Martin Gillett, Storey had been working on a study of the Lady Chapel and on completion decided to dedicate it to his brother's memory.

Mount Grace Lady Chapel: An Historical Enquiry was published later in 2001. To Storey's disappointment, a search for additional evidence had produced few results and the booklet of some 40 pages was less substantial than he had originally envisaged. Nevertheless, it was as comprehensive as possible in its treatment and outlined the Chapel's origins in the late 15th century; what happened on the site at the dissolution of the monasteries and during and after the persecutions of the later 16th century; and how Franciscans came to Osmotherley in the 1660s and had charge of the Chapel till Emancipation. Thereafter, it became the responsibility of secular clergy from Stockton and then Stokesley before falling into disuse and ruin. Following its re-discovery and the enthusiasm this evoked, the Chapel was scheduled as a national monument in 1958, the year of the first of a series of diocesan pilgrimages which have continued annually ever since. Restoration of the fabric commenced in 1959 and was followed in 1961 by formal re-dedication. In the mid-1960s the Franciscans returned to Osmotherley to preside over the Chapel, and in 1994 were succeeded by Benedictines from Ampleforth.

What Storey was unable to do for lack of evidence was to answer the question which had intrigued him for years: why did the Lady Chapel attract pilgrims over such a long period? Excavations uncovered two sets of human remains on site, and it was thought (and Storey hoped) for several years that one set might be those of Margaret Clitherow, the martyr, wife of a York butcher, who was executed under Elizabeth I. Subsequent scientific analysis ruled out this possibility, but Storey's work provides a secure starting-point for further investigation. He visited the site frequently, introduced many others to the shrine and, as we have seen, planted large numbers of trees to the north of the lane leading to it from Osmotherley. His booklet was published 'In memory of my brother, Peter Louis Storey, priest'.

The great disappointment of Storey's later years was his inability to produce the work which he longed to complete, a book on 'Relationships' or, as he put it, 'something of an autobiography of love'. After the millennium he began to suffer from age-related macular degeneration, which led to loss of sight in the centre of his visual field, and which seems in his case to have progressed relatively rapidly. Soon he ceased to be able to drive or read, and wrote only with the greatest difficulty. Inwardly, part of him raged against this disability; outwardly, he adapted remarkably well. As far as other people were concerned, his life appeared to change only marginally. Nevertheless, while others might drive him or read to him, which they did, he found no solution to his problem with writing. Despite investing in a dictaphone and the services of a commercial typing agency, he failed to make significant progress with his book. The drafts that remain, however, leave no doubt as to his lifelong debt to Aelred and Fromm. 'St. Aelred's declaration that all his life he had longed to love and be loved sent my inner self soaring on high'; and through 'my reading and study [of Fromm], my relations, my struggling and striving changed direction: the Gospel was transformed into light'.

There were other ailments. Osteoarthritis troubled him at Holy Cross, but he believed that it might be ameliorated by diet and found cider vinegar and honey helpful in his own case. He continued to travel abroad, white-water rafting at Zel Am Zee in Bavaria in July 1998 at the age of 79, and returning to Rome for a holiday in October 2001. By this stage he had begun to suspect that he had heart problems. His brother, Peter, died of heart disease in 2001 and not long afterwards tests confirmed Storey's suspicions about himself. However, his level of activity was not unduly affected. Although regularly being driven by others because of his increasing blindness, he continued to keep a very full diary, visiting Athens in 2003 and Auschwitz a year later. In 2005, in addition to long-standing commitments to various bodies - Amnesty, the Justice and Peace Commission, the Hull & District Theological Society, and the Classical Association – he invariably turned up on request at his local parish of St. Vincent's, at Holy Cross, and at St. Mary's College, and supplied across the Humber at Barton on no fewer than 11 occasions. During that year also he visited, in separate trips, Rome, Cyprus and Damascus and, in Ireland, Limerick and Derry. All this was in addition to shorter trips in Britain to visit friends, attend lectures or plant and care for his trees. When in Goddard Avenue he often shared his house with refugees and asylum seekers; and with help he kept up a large and varied correspondence.

One friend who visited him in the summer of 2006 found him in what seemed to be very good fettle. They went for a circular walk on the North York Moors to view an unusual clump of trees. Just before returning to their starting-point Storey asked to pause for five minutes to give his heart a break. This was somewhat disconcerting for his companion who, apart from the blindness, knew little else about his medical condition, but Storey was soon relaxing over a drink in the local pub, having walked five or so miles over rough ground in less than two hours.

The papers that survive from the months before his admission to hospital in early 2007 are those of a man who continued to lead an active life. Local commitments continued (weekend supplies at Barton-on-Humber for instance) with new ones appearing from time to time – an early booking was for a special Mass at Everingham in August 2007. A longer trip, planned but likewise never fulfilled, was as one of a group visiting mainland Greece, 'In the steps of St. Paul', scheduled for May 2007. In the summer of 2006 he attended a reunion at Stonyhurst, being taken there by friends from York. He engaged with Diana Johnson, his local M.P. (for Hull North) over their joint concerns about asylum seekers; and with Val Goldsack over the production of his third C.D. There was regular correspondence with at least three inmates of Hull Prison. One received legal advice and another, who had no family to support him, was sent the cost of a new pair of trainers. A third, a monk, was released on licence and Storey offered to visit him in his bolthole in the Lake District. There were letters of gratitude from people who had been helped by Storey earlier in their lives, from various locations in Britain but also from overseas. One from Uganda revealed that he had been financially supporting a small retail outlet in Kampala. A letter from Fr. Tom Rock, earlier Catholic Chaplain at Birmingham University, paid tribute to the leadership of Storey and Bruce Kent when all three had been chaplains at English universities. Until almost the very end his life remained multi-faceted and lively.

He had, however, been receiving regular medical check-ups at Castle Hill Hospital in Cottingham, where it was decided early in 2007 that he needed surgery for the replacement of a heart valve. The consultant surgeon told him at that point that one of the blood vessels close to his heart was in such a fragile state that it could burst at any moment and kill him instantly. Storey was unconcerned about death but did worry about the shock to people - in shops, the street or elsewhere – suddenly confronted by it, as had happened to him on several occasions. Having been placed on the waiting list for heart surgery at Castle Hill, he was told in mid-February that a bed would be available for him on Sunday 25th, and that surgery would take place the following day.

Although at first it was thought that the surgery had been successful, there were soon concerns about the durability of its outcome. Before long it became clear that the problem with his heart had not been resolved. Storey began to struggle and continued to do so throughout March and April. Patience, his sister, came to see him, feeling dreadfully inadequate and 'desperate for you being tied down by tubes and wires'; and (to a friend) 'I know how much he loves freedom and the outside, particularly these beautiful spring days'. Yet, while physically very ill, Storey was not cast down in spirits. He received and hugely appreciated constant and outstanding care: virtually everyone who came in contact with him at Castle Hill - doctors, nurses, auxiliaries, cleaners – knew him extremely well and had witnessed his own unfailing care of the sick. Although they were carefully monitored, there were very many visitors. He was supported throughout by a group of his close friends from Holy Cross, but ultimately to no avail. Having first asked their permission to give up the struggle, he died peacefully on 1 May 2007.

As an Ulsterman, his successor at Holy Cross, Fr. Pat Day, was used to open coffins at Irish wakes and he arranged for Storey 'to lie in state' in the church in Carrington Avenue for several days, with groups of friends and acquaintances in constant attendance. Fr. Day was thanked by one parishioner for making this time 'so happy and peaceful…to be honest, I was dreading it'. Storey had anticipated that Holy Cross might be too small to accommodate his funeral and in his will suggested, somewhat mischievously, that it might be held in the splendid medieval Anglican church of St. Mary's in Cottingham; or in St. Charles's in Jarratt Street, Hull. Following the massively attended service described at the outset of this book, he was buried in the village cemetery in Cottingham in the same grave as Fr. Thomas McEntegert, Fr. Purcell's predecessor as parish priest of Holy Cross.

CONCLUSION

Storey's ability to lead a full life until his operation, and then to withstand its after effects for over two months, demonstrated that strength and stamina were among his major assets. Beyond his sporting days this was not immediately apparent, except in the hills. Nathan Smith, a schoolboy who met Storey, then in his eighties, at Barmoor during a 'Justice & Peace' weekend, tells of climbing a nearby high point with him, Storey's dog, Shiney, and Nathan's friend, William.

> On the way up, it seemed to be a race between Shiney and Tony. Will and I were stranded, out of breath, slowly climbing up whilst Tony seemed to walk up effortlessly.

Over six feet tall Storey had longer legs than most but there was more to it than that. His physical powers could suddenly manifest themselves and startle people, as once happened to another friend:

> When he was 87 and nearly blind, I was walking with him when we came to a tall ladder stile. Rather nervously I asked, 'Will you be OK with this, Tony?', whereupon he ran up the steps and took a giant leap to land safely on the other side.

At the age of 87! Physiologically, he was something of a phenomenon, which helps to explain a good deal.

This was one reason why he coped with several demanding tasks during his curacies in Middlesbrough; why Fr. Heslin, his neighbour at Saltburn, thought him just the man to work alongside the hard taskmaster, Fr. Knowles, at St. Charles; why he got by for years on little sleep as University chaplain (though it caught up with him in the end); why he lamented the non-job at Brough Park; why activities expanded so rapidly and were sustained at Holy Cross; and why, in the midst of everything else, he was generous with the time he gave to others, read voraciously, and sustained a large correspondence. He had enormous energy and seemed to need little rest.

He was fairly highly-strung and subject to bouts of depression, which returned from time to time.

> Lovely, lovely days and a superb spring… but today is an emotional 'down' day for me for no known reason. I wonder why it is that one just senses doom and death and depression sometimes (luckily never for long) and yet is quite unable to locate the source of this.

He had a bad breakdown in Saltburn. Afterwards he concluded that one could not work round depression, but had simply to work through it, which he did; but he ran himself close to another breakdown at the end of his time as University Chaplain. Nonetheless, there were no repeats and he learned to manage his mood swings effectively, so that only close friends recognised them.

Overall, in the range and scale of what he was able to achieve, even in a long life, he was both abnormal and outstandingly successful. He came from robust stock and, except for Gerard, the war casualty, Storey and all his siblings were long-lived, with John surviving him into his nineties.

Once they flew the nest they were very independent, seeing each other and their parents infrequently, only partly because of dislocation, and yet always available for help or advice. Storey was candid about the distance between himself and his father during his childhood. George Storey had a huge job amidst the agricultural difficulties of the inter-war period, and yet Storey always paid tribute to the influence of his father's historical knowledge and interests. Like other parents of large families, George and Harriet developed a shared system. By the time Storey came along, George concentrated on the older boys and Harriet dealt primarily with the younger boys and the girls. Luckily, Storey was able to compensate for the imbalance in his case when circumstances brought father and youngest son physically much closer together during George's final years at Everingham. His comments about both parents were very positive.

Agatha's were not. For one person at least, the atmosphere in the Storey household was not good. In middle-age certainly, Agatha bitterly resented the distance and tension which developed between her parents after Storey's birth as they sought to avoid repeated pregnancies. The evidence is sparse and comes from a period when Agatha did not have her troubles to seek. Her sufferings were probably not shared, or at least not shared to the same extent, by the older brothers; and they appear to have come as something of a surprise to Storey himself. Though she got on with them all, Agatha was somewhat isolated, being for many years the only girl, sharing a bedroom with her mother after Storey's birth; and her only sister, Patience, was seven years younger than him. This large family of strong-minded individuals was not particularly close-knit. What did unite them, solidly and imperviously, was their religious belief. All the evidence, including intimate correspondence from John and Patience at the end of Storey's life, is that Catholicism was the bedrock of their existence and the cement in their relationship, something which, despite their very different lives, never altered.

Storey owed a great deal to Harriet, who taught him his faith and laid the educational basis of his later academic success. Like many people, he learned best in a sympathetic environment among teachers to whom he could relate. He found Bishop's Court and the Gregorian unimpressive and somewhat uncongenial, but blossomed at Stonyhurst. There, students were encouraged and helped to develop as far as they could. Besides having lots of opportunity for sport, which he loved, he obtained his school certificates remarkably quickly; and then in the Higher Religious Certificate found an intellectual cum physical activity for which he had great aptitude, and through which he exhibited presentational skills which were admired, which he honed, and which ultimately were of a very high order indeed. It was his experience of the Higher Religious Certificate which underpinned one of his chief characteristics: a determination while being deeply committed to his faith to get to the bottom of anything relating to it, so that he understood it thoroughly and could articulate it clearly. In proceeding to the English College he cited a desire to see the Christian faith renewed. This wish may have germinated at home among his family, but it was reared at Stonyhurst.

Later his carefully cultivated fluency in matters of his faith made him a valued presence among Christians of all denominations, but early in his career it sometimes got him into trouble - for instance, with Fr. McMullan at St. Joseph's in 1950 over the question of the definition of the dogma of the Assumption, and again later with *Humanae Vitae.* He found it very difficult, at times impossible, to accept anything which he regarded as inappropriate or incorrect. We do not know the issues on which his frank comments nearly got him expelled, twice, from the English College, but there is little evidence of his suppressing his views in later years. It was never his style to go on the warpath with his opinions; he respected those of others. Nor, however, did he lapse into silence; or, more to the point, fail to ensure that his convictions informed his ministry.

His feelings about the English College were different from those about the Gregorian. Despite (along with many others) being critical of teaching at the University, he enjoyed his time at the College. He made some close and lasting friendships. He got to know many parts of Italy, afterwards always a favourite destination, along with virtually every nook and cranny of Rome. At a time of international tension his experiences there were educative, to say the least. And it was there that he began keeping up-to-date with developments at the centre of the Church, a pursuit which he sustained throughout his life. Nevertheless, by far the most startling feature of these seminary years was the step-change in his intellectual development which followed his move from Rome to St. Mary's Hall. Being taught in English on familiar ground, by scholars who did not look for mere regurgitation of what he had absorbed, produced not only an enthusiasm for theological study which previously had not been evident; but also a growing interest in political theory, sociology and related matters. The transition in 1940 from a 'phoney' to a 'hot' war was also influential, putting everyone on their mettle. At the Gregorian he had not looked forward to his classes. At St. Mary's he did. For his last year, 1942-43, he was appointed Senior Student, certain evidence of a positive attitude.

And yet until merely days before the event he remained unsure whether to proceed to priestly ordination. Unlike his brother Peter, Storey had not been singled out at home as a possible future priest; he was not so regarded at Stonyhurst and seems to have been discreet about his intentions until just before he left; and, unusually, he remained uncertain about his vocation throughout his seven years of philosophy and theology. The critical meeting with Fr. Agnellus Andrew which resolved his dilemma was an extraordinary episode, but its importance lies less in the manner of the resolution than in the impact it had on Storey. Henceforward he never entertained the slightest doubt about his role in life. Absolute certainty repeatedly brought freshness and vigour to his priesthood. Intellectually and spiritually he moved resolutely forward, seeking constantly to identify the best way ahead but never fundamentally unsure of his route or of his objective.

It is no wonder that he hugely enjoyed his years in Cambridge. He was presented with opportunities to play seriously competitive rugby, this time under experienced coaches, among keen players, and ultimately as Captain of Christ College's First XV. In the Milton Society he was able further to develop his love of debating. Between these pastimes and his studies he had early pastoral engagement with allied servicemen and, while doing so, explored the fenland landscape which was new to him. Above all, for three years he was free to read, talk, think and write. He knew that he was lucky and made the most of it, needing no encouragement to range intellectually very widely indeed. His degree course revealed how, since the fall of the Roman Empire, the whole of Europe had developed and he found it stimulating to study this in wartime when so many past achievements were threatened. In later years he slightly revised this judgement: the prime value of his course, he came to feel, lay in having rounded out and complemented both his previous and his later theological studies. A totally fortuitous bonus was his engagement with Dom David Knowles, who involved him closely in the writings of Aelred of Rievaulx, which provided a wellspring for the rest of his life. A final benefit of these years was the sharp contrast between social life in a seminary and in a university. At Cambridge he 'began to make very good relationships with all sorts of people'.

Subsequently, there was yet another formative influence, arguably the most important of all – his encounter as a curate with the poor working class of two of northern England's most deprived areas. While he eagerly anticipated his first experience of parish work, he was also apprehensive. There were things about himself that he could not disguise: his plummy accent, his impeccable manners, his gentlemanly demeanour. At a time when the British class system remained very strong, it was obvious to everyone that he came from a different social class from those to whom he was to minister. Would they accept him? And if not, what was he to do about it? To his huge relief, they did so unreservedly, recognising integrity when they saw it. He grew to love them, for this perhaps above all else, and they loved him in return. Here was someone who, despite his background, not only said Mass for them, absolved them, baptised their babies and buried their dead; he also visited them in their homes and in hospital; he hung out their washing and lit their fires when they were unable to do so themselves; he paid the cost of attending a retreat for at least one parishioner who could not afford it, and no doubt there were others; and he was prepared when the need arose to wash and lay out their dead.

Although he appears to have had little difficulty in adjusting to life in Middlesbrough, it took him several years to shed some of the attitudes of the rural upper middle class into which he was born. As late as his debating days at Christ's College, some of his views owed more to his past than to his future. In Middlesbrough, however, he worked, albeit briefly, with the resilient, ebullient Irishman, Fr. Paddy McEnroe; he also mixed with members of the Young Christian Worker movement, engagement with whom was mutually rewarding; and given his fresh pastoral experience, and having earlier been sceptical of the new Labour government's plans, he applauded the foundation of the National Health Service and the implementation of other recommendations of the Beveridge Report. He was influenced by all these experiences, especially mixing regularly with ordinary people, and became less conservative and more radical in his attitudes. Moreover, in Hull he encountered even greater poverty and deprivation than on Teesside. He was not just taken aback by the living conditions of many people there: he was shocked and at times deeply depressed by them. He steered clear of party politics, for which he never had much time, but came to describe himself eventually as a liberal on the left. Undoubtedly, it was in these two urban areas that he established a personal preference for the poor, so evident in his later ministry, and subsequently he never lost sight of this priority.

Another never-to-be-forgotten lesson as a curate was the imperative of absolute respect for the individual in dealing with the mentally deficient or disturbed. Later, in his memoir and on big set-piece occasions such as his retirement from Cottingham, he paid tribute to what he had learned from Dr. Cuthbert at the Cleveland Mental Hospital. From then on these lessons permeated his counselling and ultimately he came to the conclusion that 'almost all mental illness is spiritual'. It was not just a matter of making the correct approach to patients, profoundly important though this was. It might also be necessary to summon the courage to change an entire system radically in pursuit of the common good. We should bear this in mind when considering his re-ordering of the churches at Stokesley and Cottingham, where he pressed ahead in the face of some fierce opposition. At the same time Storey was honest enough to acknowledge that he made mistakes and learned from them, notably those involved in his work with the diocesan Rescue Society: in permanently separating mothers and babies at birth, and in not insisting that the facts of their birth be made clear to adopted children.

In its significance, however, nothing compared with the book he discovered during his early years at St. Charles, *The Art of Loving* by Erich Fromm. Once he had read it alongside Aelred's treatise 'On Spiritual Friendship' he became acutely aware of a yawning gap between reality and the Church's approach to affective relationships. This permanently informed his counselling and his personal relations with both sexes. It seems idiosyncratic to have coupled a 12th-century abbot with a 20th-century social philosopher, psychoanalyst and atheist. However, clues from his early life suggest why Storey did so. He was troubled by guilt from the time he made his first confession and later particularly regretted the bullying he was responsible for at Bishop's Court and Stonyhurst. Quite when the following occurred we do not know, but 'it was….my discovery of Julian of Norwich which freed me from hangover guilt': it was she who persuaded him that guilt was self-regarding, whereas sorrow looked to God. Viewed in this light, every fall was a growth point for the future. Long before he was freed from hangover guilt, however, Storey became critical of the way in which moral questions were dealt with by theologians. Many of those at the Gregorian were narrow-minded and pessimistic. As in seminaries elsewhere, conventions at the English College were not much different, positively discouraging 'special friendships', with students being instructed not to sit regularly next to the same person in the Common Room or elsewhere; and never to go out into the city in ones and twos, but always in groups of at least three. Aelred's treatise advocated a quite different approach: close personal friendships were not only acceptable but potentially helpful if one wanted to progress in the spiritual life. The question arose as to why such a wide gap had opened up between this medieval thinking and current orthodoxy. It was Fromm who provided the answer. People felt a strong need to love and be loved but, aiding and abetting prohibitions accumulated over the ages, no part of their education (and certainly no part of Storey's) was devoted to learning how to do so. Henceforward he spent much time and energy in helping himself and others to bridge this gap: it was precisely because he had to help himself in this respect that he was so successful in helping others.

For him this was a period of great change. The second half of his life was in important respects very different from the first. 'I only really started to *think* in the late 1950s and the explosion of the 1960s' - hyperbolic perhaps, but indicative of a significant shift in outlook. Although there is only broad chronological evidence to go on, it may not have been co-incidental that it was at about this time - following his move from Middlesbrough to Hull - that his relationship with M. deepened. These were also the years when he became conversant with the marital difficulties of his parents. He saw with absolute clarity the sharp contradiction in having been taught not to relate to women and his pastoral duty to prepare people for marriage. Thereafter, he never ceased to equip himself to discharge this duty effectively, spending much time with those in difficulties, being as constructive as possible in cases of marital breakdown, and reaching his own conclusions in cases where he felt evidence was clear-cut regarding the question of whether individuals might subsequently receive Holy Communion. As a chaplain at the University and St. Mary's College he worked hard to ensure that students developed a sound attitude to their sexuality, insisting that no attempt be made to shield them from the information they required in order to take their own decisions; but at the same time firmly extolling the virtue of chastity until such time as commitment became permanent.

The Second Vatican Council constituted another personal watershed. No-one expected an elderly Pope, elected as a compromise candidate, to summon a Council. Storey was delighted and excited; and having clearly identified two of Pius XII's early encyclicals as ground-breaking – not a judgement made by many – he hoped to see the issues they raised pursued still further. It was his good fortune that his appointment as University Chaplain was followed so closely by the opening of the Council. It had long been his custom to keep abreast of what happened in Rome. This was particularly appropriate in his new position, where he was surrounded by educated Catholic staff and students, eager for news and interpretation; not to mention members of other denominations, some of whom were scarcely less interested. Storey followed everything, acquired copies of the Council documents as soon as they became available, studied them carefully, and frequently returned to them. It was an intensely interesting period when very many pressing issues facing the Church were confronted, deliberated and decided upon. The Council constituted a key juncture in the evolution of his life as a priest.

He could not have been more satisfied with the scope of the Council's deliberations. The laity were given a central position as the people of God in the constitution of the Church. The liturgical changes which were the subject of a separate decree, particularly the introduction of the vernacular, served to emphasise and enhance their position. The decree on religious freedom, establishing conscience as the ultimate arbiter, confronted tyranny in all its guises, but was also relevant internally, supporting individuals like Storey in continuing to apply their minds to the subject of their faith. Ecumenism was freed from the shackles of prejudice and Catholics were challenged to understand and respect the beliefs of others, Christians and non-Christians alike. Unlike most others, the Council's programme was so large and its outcomes so revolutionary that the agenda for implementation would inevitably have been substantial even if its decrees had been universally welcomed, which they were not. Storey spent the rest of his priestly life working on this agenda: liturgically, translating the Council's decisions into parochial practice and urging his parishioners to espouse them wholeheartedly; and intellectually, publishing his views on the priesthood of the faithful, 'Collaborative Ministry', only shortly before his death. He was keenly aware of those like his brother, Peter, who regarded the Council's deliberations as misguided, but was never cast down by such views. In his judgement the outcomes of the Council were like 'a smouldering volcano' which would eventually carry all before them.

By the mid-1960s most Catholics were in a positive mood. While Vatican II's decisions had not met with universal approval, the younger generation in particular had responded enthusiastically. This mood was shattered by Paul VI's encyclical *Humanae Vitae*. Against the background of his parents' and his own pastoral experience, Storey was shocked. His response was typical of the man. He discussed the issues widely and openly, he did not over react, he thought long and hard, and he wrote down his considered views in a draft article. He then sent this draft to his bishop, asking for advice about possible publication which, predictably and understandably in the midst of the furore, was to hold off. Storey contemplated the possibility of having to stand down in some way if the national Bishops' Conference took a hard line: but he suspected, correctly, that this would not be the case. However, he did not try to hide behind silence, as would have been possible, but let his superior know his position exactly – the honourable thing to do.

Athough Storey never easily moved from a position which he had thought through, he eventually changed his stance in another area: as University Chaplain following the troubles at Hull around the turn of the 1960s. Having established the welfare of students as his priority - and this would have been carefully considered – he began to ponder this decision in 1967, i.e. before the events of 1968 and beyond. He felt that many students had too easily neglected, albeit perhaps temporarily, principles and values to which they had once adhered and to which he believed they should hold fast. The subsequent constitutional difficulties with the University authorities broadened this spirit of rejection;

and it became clear, as the chaplains' statement spelled out, that the situation had been exploited to the point where rational discussion became impossible. The University continued to operate simply because of the powers of endurance of those in charge, with whom Storey felt great sympathy. He stood out publicly against what happened and concluded that the welfare of the University as a whole should have been his prime concern all along. Few criticised him, but he took these developments very badly; along with his car crash and general exhaustion, they reduced him to the fragile state in which his successor found him in the late summer of 1972.

The nine years which followed were among his most difficult. The two Storey brothers were well aware of contrasts in their attitudes: according to widespread testimony, they were as different as chalk from cheese. They had co-incided physically for any length of time during two periods only - at home when Storey himself was a child and young boy, and for four years or so at the English College. As priests they worked in different parts of the diocese, Peter largely in the north, and Storey largely in the south, and saw each other occasionally and often unpredictably. By 1973 it was perhaps too early for anyone, even themselves, to realise just how differently they felt about the outcomes of Vatican II. So when one followed the other as parish priest in Stokesley it proved problematical through no fault of either of them. The diocese acknowledged at his death that Storey had been exceedingly unhappy to have been moved to Brough Park in 1979 following receipt of a letter from his brother, recently appointed Vicar General. At the time his unhappiness was well-known among his fellow clergy. For Storey, however, Fr. Peter's involvement was a temporary irritant – that was the way things sometimes were with Vicars General; more serious was the absence of a significant task at Brough Park.

If this episode constituted 'a dark night' for Storey's soul, as one senior diocesan colleague suggested, it didn't take long for him to recover. He sought and warmly welcomed the challenge of his appointment to Holy Cross. There he galvanised and transformed the parish, made an abiding impression on the entire Christian community, and together with his parishioners did valuable work overseas. Lots of people benefited, not least himself. By this stage of his life he had largely left behind the mood swings of earlier years. At the golden jubilee of his ordination in 1993 when he was 74 years old, he felt able to proclaim that he came 'towards the last lap with an ever deepening joy'.

As a newly ordained priest, he had set out with 'immense hope'. Now, towards the end of his ministry, the same message of hope remained 'the ground of my preaching'. He had come to realise that 'the good news of the gospel was not conditional but absolute'. Most significantly for our understanding of him, he went on to articulate how his love of nature had become bound up with the development of his theology. 'The whole universe is the word of God being said, moment by moment....the whole creation is now enfolded in him who creates it'. His care for the environment, therefore, had not been merely a personal pre-occupation: whether or not he had realised it as a young man, it had been a tribute to 'a world, a universe, shot through with the Divine'. The naturalist nurtured in him from his earliest years at Warter, his deep love of trees and his care for them and everything else in the environment, reflected 'the glory [which] now fills all heaven and earth'. We do not know when he arrived at this conviction - neither perhaps did he - but there is no doubt that the writings of Teilhard de Chardin, the French Jesuit and palaeontologist, were a major influence. As early as November 1968 he was 'once again immersed in reading Teilhard and, as always, have that intense sense of elan and excitement in his synthetic approach to all creation'. Another influence during

Storey's retirement was the Dalai Lama, who he heard speak in Belfast.

> The great lesson of the Dalai Lama…is that the sense of the holy is catholic, but far wider than Catholic. The cosmic Christ presence is a deep truth.

In this key sense Storey's theology became universal.

Central to his experience as a priest, he testified, was the revolution in the Church's understanding of priesthood: the people of God were all involved, every single one of them. He rejoiced in this. He was also delighted by the Church's acceptance of the need to be separate from the state, a conviction nurtured during his days in Mussolini's Italy. Nor is it fanciful to suggest that the Church's clear proclamation of the need for freedom of religion and of conscience went right back to his days with the Jesuits at Stonyhurst. In his mature view 'all these four aspects of Catholic life are still *in via,* are struggling for birth, are subject to immense tensions within the Church, but will be the established position in the next century'.

According to his own testimony, among the convictions which had grown in him during his pastoral work was 'the primacy of persons', who had to be engaged with 'where they are': it was useless for him to start from where he was. This did not mean, however, that he could operate without constraint. In a long succession of posts his primary duty had been 'to serve'; if on occasion he felt bound 'to protest', he had to be prepared, ultimately, 'to obey'. Among his duties he always regarded preparation for marriage as of immense importance - one of his primary ministries. He married countless couples and remained committed to them. He believed that one should never run away from cases of marital difficulty or breakdown. In such cases and when dealing with the mentally ill, it was necessary to be fearless, imaginative and as deeply informed as one could be. He had ceased to worry about the endless interruptions to a priest's life. Striving for perfection was unhelpful because, at least in his own experience, it created anger. In seeking to serve and in striving to be fatherly, creative and loving, nothing was to be regarded as too menial.

Towards the end of his life Storey made it crystal clear that, in pursuing his vocation, he had found it immensely helpful to treat men and women equally.

> I have, as I have aged and I hope matured, a huge number of friends, men and women, which always brings joy when we meet or are in touch, but I would say that I have about not more than 15 real friends. By that I mean fellow spirits with whom there is nothing consciously barred, whose presence is sheer peace, and with whom conversation and exchange is without the least inhibition. I could name 15 such, ten of whom are women.

With both men and women there was deep affection, total trust, and neither demands nor conditions. Sexual activity did not belong in such friendships because either one or both were already committed: that too made for 'a wonderful freedom'. Eventually, along with everything else which gave him a sense of satisfaction, he arrived at a point where there was no dichotomy between his priesthood and his manhood.

To turn to the question raised at the outset, why was Storey never promoted beyond a parish priesthood: to, say, a Canon, a Monsignor or something further? It is helpful to recall his own view of himself. In the uncompleted draft of his proposed book on 'Relationships', he revealed that 'I've always felt slightly on the outside of things'. He elaborated this a little in his dictated memoir when dealing with the decisive interview with Fr. Agnellus Andrew prior to his ordination. 'I never really found myself enamoured of the clerical set up, I must say, and so I always felt slightly an outsider'. Another version of this line of thinking appeared as early as 1965. 'I have always been anti-cleric[al] and I find much in the juridical set-up of the Church most unpleasing, but Catholic doctrine and moral teaching has [sic] always seemed to me to be sheer sense, and the more I have to defend it, discuss it and argue about it, the more it seems to be sense'. There was never the slightest danger of this cleric succumbing to clericalism.

He was different from many clergy and not merely in terms of his background and education. Particularly when relaxed, he had a zany sense of humour, sometimes behaved eccentrically, and was given to marvellous flights of fancy. Reporting on a visit by Storey to his workshop, a friend's son, a woodworker, said:

> A lovely man – saw everything and met everyone. Mind you, he is a bit strange. Outside, just before he left, he began dancing and singing on top of our tree trunks.

For Storey this was normal, even characteristic, though startling to anyone unaware of his love affair with trees. He liked to play around with the English language. The words 'putative father' were first commonly used in the 1960s. He soon invented, and then used disparagingly, the verb 'to pute'. Among his favourite words was 'great', but with at least three or four 'rs' between the 'g' and the 'e'. Camping by Lake Garda in baking heat, Storey spied someone selling ice cream from a boat. He ran down to the shoreline shouting 'Grrreat Ice Cream, Grrreat Ice Cream!' For days afterwards, as he plied his trade, the Italian boatman could be heard employing the same refrain. It was perhaps behaviour of this kind which led to Storey first being described to Fr. Pat Day as 'a strange priest, a bit of a looney'. This was grossly incorrect, of course, but one can imagine what might have provoked the remark.

Nor is there much doubt that his growing involvement with Amnesty International and his burgeoning interest in third-world issues led some of his fellow clergy, and some laity, to mark him down as a left-winger. In 1982, having been given a blue Shetland pullover, Storey felt that it:

> may assuage the graver and more balanced parishioners who are now beginning openly to reject my (evidently Russian-financed) left-wing pacifist views. Much better to be dead than red, one said to me today.

According to Fr. John Bane, who later assisted him at Holy Cross, 'although Fr. Tony was viewed as a left-wing maverick by many clergy of the time, I did not find him so'. In fact and unsurprisingly, grumbles about the nature and tenor of some of his activities were evident during his chaplaincy days; and in 1970, in supporting a younger colleague who wished to study at Oxford, Storey wrote of himself being labelled as an intellectual 'and quite overtly spoken of as a threat and a danger'. He went on to be severely critical of the diocesan record in regard to educating its priests.

It is difficult to judge how much, if any, of this might have prevented a promotion. In many respects he was quite different from the bulk of his fellow clergy. He came from a different social class, was far better educated, developed outstanding presentational skills, and could hold his own in any company. He was indeed an intellectual and it showed. All these traits may have made him suspect in some quarters, but would have been more likely to win him promotion (as they did for his brother, Fr. Peter) than to prevent it. Some negative comment was mere tittle-tattle: gossip was irritating but there was no means of preventing it. Some was mere prejudice. Storey did not himself put a silver spoon in his mouth; and indeed came to the view on grounds of equality that the public schools should be phased out. Some was plainly wrong. Certainly, anyone who felt that Storey's broadly liberal views were evidence of softness was profoundly mistaken. As University Chaplain he challenged students, individually and collectively, if he felt that they were being complacent, thoughtless or unprincipled. Among other possible considerations were health issues. Storey was known to have suffered a breakdown and to be subject to bouts of depression. On the other hand few clergy were generally as fit and healthy as he was. If anything counted strongly against him it was likely to have been his progressive views on theological matters. His more conservative superiors and colleagues could easily have regarded him as not 'sound'. While never loud-mouthed, he made little attempt to conceal his views. His bishop was promptly informed of his opinion of *Humanae Vitae*, adherence to which under Pope John Paul II was regarded as one of the pillars of orthodoxy, and which in this case *may* have been a crunch issue. Storey's consolation, if he needed any, was that he too regarded it as a crunch issue and was content to pay the price for it being so.

There are two other possible lines of interpretation. He may have been sheltered. Aware of his independent cast of mind and his fearlessness in the face of what he believed to be the truth of a matter, he may have been left at a certain level in order to safeguard him from higher authority. He was clearly free to operate in the way that he chose: not merely to criticise the revised code of canon law, but even, in the case of his letter to *The Tablet* of October 1998 (by which time of course he had retired), to outline pastoral practice on his part which was (and remains) unorthodox.

An alternative and more plausible explanation is that it was Storey himself who exercised the greatest influence on what happened to him. In March 1972, having chaired a two-day conference of University chaplains in Durham:

I found it left me all nervy and tense, and I realise I could never be a politician or a headmaster or in any position demanding hard clear leadership and authority. I'm for Mull and crofting every time.

We do not know whether he was offered promotion and, if so, in what form; nor do we know his response. Most of those who knew Storey well find it difficult to believe that he would have welcomed promotion: either titularly (that might have compromised his independence) or more substantially (ditto and in any case he was a people person, not a desk man). Two things seem abundantly clear. He would certainly not have sacrificed his views to the system; and despite earlier misguided and mistaken grumbles, both his superiors and the diocesan clergy admired and respected him in later years. As for the laity, very few people came into contact with him for any length of time without feeling that they had encountered someone very special indeed. As one of his close friends put it at his death:

Storey was an amazing person, always thinking things through uncompromisingly, following what he thought was true, and yet his sense of the sacred and of traditional values still shone through.

He was a priest for his time.

Note on Sources

The diocesan archives in Middlesbrough hold records of all the parishes to which Storey was attached, beginning with those of SS. Mary & Joseph in Pocklington at the time of his birth. There is a set of the diocesan *Almanac & Directory* which not only annually records official details of his career but also contains several short articles by him. There are boxes of his personal papers found in Goddard Avenue at the time of his death. Voluminous and uncatalogued, these nevertheless contain invaluable material, notably two uncompleted drafts (one short and one rather longer) of the book on 'Relationships' which he began towards the end of his life: these are revealing but difficult to read, being very poorly constructed from his dictation (box 2, bundle 5). Amid much else there are papers relating to the WEA course he delivered in 1958-59 (box 7, file 1); the letter of December 1967 revealing his growing disenchantment with aspects of student life (box 1, bundle 5); correspondence from the early 1990s about the design of a new Health & Sex Education policy at St. Mary's College (box 4, file 2); and many papers relating to his broadcasting activities during his later years (box 7, file 5). The diocese also holds a long series of copies of the Hull Catholic Magazine in which, under the editorship of Fr. J. Knowles, Storey was prominent while a curate at St. Charles.

However, much of the evidence on which this book is based has been drawn from private sources which are not readily accessible. It would be confusing and perhaps invidious to provide references to material which is accessible but not to that which is not: hence this Note. The single most significant source is a personal memoir, running to some 41 A4 pages, dictated by Storey to Susan Frost in 2005, which is particularly revealing of his childhood, upbringing and early schooling, but also of much else beyond his early years. Ultimately, having reached the 1970s, Storey was sufficiently unimpressed by this, judging it to be too anecdotal, to leave it incomplete: but it is richly informative, particularly when examined alongside the formal records at Stonyhurst and the English College in Rome. In the case of the former the meticulous reports compiled about events at the College yield much information not just about Storey himself but also about his teachers and colleagues. The dramatic wartime developments which engulfed his generation at the English College feature prominently in the memoir: but they were also recorded by his contemporaries, both as they happened and in a series of retrospective essays in the College house magazine, The Venerabile. Where records are sparse, as at Christ's College, Cambridge, Storey's memoir leaves no doubt that this utterly unanticipated educational opportunity constituted one of the key turning-points in his life.

Once he became immersed in parochial and diocesan life, the evidence expands and becomes less formal and more varied. There is a steadily growing volume from parishioners and others among whom he worked, as well as personal papers, including correspondence. In large measure this material has been supplied by his friends, principally and substantially by Marian Hall, who Storey named as his 'next of kin'. Other significant evidence has come from Margaret Blatchford (the festschrift presented to him by students in 1972, together with other information regarding his last years as University Chaplain); Christina Lucey (miscellaneous correspondence, especially while he was at Brough Park and Bedale); Emrys Hughes (miscellaneous correspondence and the text of Storey's address to the legal fraternity in York Minster in 1990); and Teresa Ulyatt (who has a large collection of newsletters and parish council papers from Holy Cross, Cottingham). Parishioners there responded generously to an invitation to write to me about their experience of Storey as parish priest, and Carole and Jim Appleby, his next-door neighbours in Goddard Avenue, shared their memories of his years of retirement. It is hoped that the bulk of the material in private hands will ultimately be lodged in a single major archive.

Bibliography

Allen, D. *St. Joseph's, Stokesley: The Story of a Catholic Parish* (Stockton, 1972).

Bamford, T.W. *The University of Hull: the First Fifty Years* (Oxford, 1978)

Briggs, A. *Victorian Cities* (London, 1963)

- 'Public Health: The Sanitary Idea', *New Society,* 281 (1968), 229-231

Brooke, C.N.L. *A History of the University of Cambridge* IV *1870-1990* (Cambridge, 1993)

- - *David Knowles Remembered* (Cambridge, 1991)

Buxton, W. 'Last Boat from Le Havre', *The Venerabile,* 29 (1990), 12-16

Carson, R. *The First 100 Years: A History of the Diocese of Middlesbrough 1878-1998* (Middlesbrough, 1998)

Clark, A. 'Exodus, 1940', *The Venerabile,* 9 (1940), 391-404

Collingwood, L. 'Corpus Christi (Middlesbrough) New Church', *Diocesan Almanac & Directory* (1950), 99

Cornforth, J. 'Brough Hall, Yorkshire – The Seat of Sir Ralph Lawson Bt.', *Country Life,* 142 (1967), 894-898 & 948-952

Cottingham & District Leader, 12 February 1993

Dove, A. *Touched by God* (Dublin, 2012)

Duffy, E. *Saints and Sinners: A History of the Popes* (4th edn. London, 2014)

Dyos, H.J. & Wolff, M. *The Victorian City: Images & Realities* 2 Vols. (London 1973)

Fromm, E. *The Art of Loving* (London, 1956)

Frostick, E. *The Story of Hull and Its People* (Hull, 1990)

Gillett, C. & McMahon, K.A. *A History of Hull* (2nd & extended edn. Oxford, 1989)

Grogan, P. '1940: Exiles on Their Own Shores', *The Venerabile,* 29 (1990), 7-11

Haltemprice Advertiser, 4 November 1993

Hastings, A. *A History of English Christianity* (London, 1986)

Hull Catholic Magazine ed. Rev. J. Knowles, Jan-Feb 1956 to Oct-Nov 1962

Killeen, M. *A Tender Love* (Ingleton, 2009)

Lavery, H. 'The Ambleside Episode', *The Venerabile,* 9 (1940), 406-413

- - 'Jubilee 1943-93', *The Venerabile,* 30 (1995), 115-118

Leonard, J.W. 'City Beautiful: Planning the Future in Mid-Twentieth-Century Middlesbrough' in Pollard, A.J. ed. *Middlesbrough: Town and Community 1830-1950* (Stroud, 1996)

Lillie, W. *The History of Middlesbrough: An Ilustration of the Evolution of English Industry* (Middlesbrough, 1968)

Lyons, J. & Furnival, I. eds. *Fiftieth Anniversary of the Cross-Carrying Pilgrimage July 1948-1998* (Liverpool, n.d.)

Mack Smith, D. *Modern Italy: A Political History* (London, 1997)

Markham, I. *The Church of St. Charles Borromeo, Hull* (Beverley, 2014)

Memorial Issue: Fr. Antony Storey 1919-2007 R.I.P. Diocese of Middlesbrough Justice & Peace Commission (2007)

Milburn, D. 'Father Hugh Lavery', *The Venerabile,* 30 (1995), 119-120

Minskip, D. *St. Joseph's R.C. Church Middlesbrough, with some personal memories by Fr. J. Anthony Barry* (Middlesbrough, n.d.)

Muir, T.E. *Stonyhurst* (rev. edn. Stonyhurst, 2006)

Murphy-O'Connor, C. *An English Spring: Memoirs* (London, 2016)

O'Malley, *The Jesuits: A History from Ignatius to the Present* (Washington, 2014)

Pevsner, N. York and the East Riding (London, 1972)

Philpot, T. *A Short History of Palazzola* (Rome, 2001)

Powicke, F.M. ed. *Walter Daniel's Life of Ailred, Abbot of Rievaulx* (London, 1950)

Race, M. *A Century of Care: A History of St. Luke's Hospital, Middlesbrough* (Middlesbrough, 1998)

Ravenstern, E.V. 'The Laws of Migration', *Journal of the Royal Statistical Society,* XLVIII (1885)

Rimmer, J.A. *The Village that was Formby* (Freshfield, 2007)

Seeds Southport & District Directory 1927-28 (Preston, 1927)

- - - - - *1930-31* (Preston, 1930)

Sigsworth, E. 'Homes Unfit for Heroes', *Yorkshire Post,* 5 July 1962

Sire, H. *Fr. Martin D'Arcy: Philosopher of Christian Love* (London, 1997)

Stonyhurst Magazine

Storey, A.J. 'A Patron for a Dalesman', *Diocesan Almanac & Directory* (1948), 96-97

- 'Our Lady's Chapel at Mount Grace, *Diocesan Almanac & Directory* (1956), 116-117

- - 'What is a Martyr?', *Diocesan Almanac & Directory* (1961), 125-126

- - 'Father Knowles: A Personal Memoir', *Hull Catholic Magazine,* Feb-Mar 1964, 14, 17-18

- 'St. Joseph's, Stokesley', *Diocesan Almanac & Directory* (1975), 53

- 'New Law Contrary to Natural Justice', *The Times,* 11 February

1984

- 'Marriage in Holy Writ: A Development of Doctrine', *Priests and People*, (September 1987), 208-209
- 'Our Easter Hope and My Priesthood', *Priests and People,* (April 1993), 145-147
- 'I Was There: The 14th Station', Part I, *Middlesbrough Catholic Voice,* July 1998, 3, 6
- 'The March to Walsingham: The 14th Station', Part II, *Middlesbrough Catholic Voice,* August 1998, 5
- 'Letter', *The Tablet,* 31 October 1998
- *Mount Grace Lady Chapel: An Historical Enquiry* (Beverley, 2001)
- 'On Collaborative Ministry', *The Furrow,* 58, No. 1 (Jan 2007), 58-60

Sweeney, G. *St. Edmund's House, Cambridge: the First Eighty Years* (Cambridge, 1980)

Walsh, M. *St. Edmund's College, Cambridge, 1896-1996: A Commemorative History* (Cambridge, 1996)

Warwick, T. *Central Middlesbrough through Time* (Stroud, 2013)

Wilkinson, J. 'Six Decades in the Priesthood', *Hull & East Yorkshire Mail,* 26 April 2003, 2-3

Williams, M.E. *The Venerable English College, Rome: A History* (2nd edn. Leominster, 2008)

Yorke, B. *Formby and Freshfield in Times Past* (Chorley, 1987)
- & R. *Images of England: Formby, Freshfield & Altcar* (Stroud, 1999)

Picture Acknowledgements

Marian Hall: Front cover, Frontispiece, 2-6, 9-17, 21-30.
Middlesbrough Diocesan Archives: 19, 20.
Stonyhurst College: 7, 8.
Teresa Ulyatt 18.

Index

CAFOD 178, 190, 194, 196, 200
Camara, Dom Helder 196
Cambridge 157, 162
-   Addenbrooke's Hospital 86-8
 - University 83, 228
-   Benet House 82
-   Christ's College 4, 6-7, 81-84,
    87-89, 94, 99, 153, 229
-   Peterhouse 94, 96
-   Sidney Sussex College 84
-   St. Edmund's House 82-84, 87,
    99
-   St. John's College 93
-   Trinity Hall 85
Canada 34, 71
Carnforth 170
Carr, John 16
Case, Fred 171-72
Catholic Action 47, 55, 97, 107, 114
Catholic Evidence Guild 46, 107,
    131
Catholic Holiday Guild 70
Catholic Marriage Advisory Council
    139
Chadwick, Canon John 119-122,
    130
Chamberlain, Neville 21, 65, 67
Charlemagne 159
Cherry-Garrard, Apsley 60
Chi Lo Sa 61-62, 69, 71
Chile 196
Christ the King 47-48
Cicero 94
Clark, Fr. Ernest 38
Classical Association 219
Clitherow, St. Margaret 174, 218
Cologne 80, 159

Communism 101
Constable family 16, 181
Connolly, Kevin 147
Cook, Monica 210
Cooper family 28
Corpus Christi, Feast of 46
 - College 173-74
Cottingham 21, 184-85, 209-10, 222
 - Pa. of Holy Cross 12, 184, 219-
    20, 222, 224, 235-36
 - Parish Council 186-91, 208
 - Building 186-89, 230
 - Catechesis 192
 - Christian Aid 193
 - Churches Together 209
 - Ecumenism 190, 193
 - Groups 191-93, 200, 201, 210
 - Magazine 190
 - Priory Room 190, 193-94
 - St. Mary's (Anglican) 185, 222
 - Third World Projects 190, 195-
    199
 - Traidcraft 195
 - Youth Club 192
 - Castle Hill Hospital 185, 192,
    200, 203, 209, 221-22
 - De La Pole Hospital 185, 209
Coughlan, Fr. Kevin 125, 127-29
Coulton, Professor G.C. 93
Crete 202
Crisell, Peter 171
Crosby 30
Crowley, Bishop John 208, 210
Cuban Missile Crisis 153
Cuthbert, Dr. T.M. 111-12, 230
Cyprus 220

249

253

255

257